GOD'S PLAN
REVEALED

By
Robert C. Luisi Jr.

Scriptures are taken from NKJV & Amplified Version Bible

BY FAITH WE UNDERSTAND

Now faith is the substance of things hoped for, the evidence of things not seen. For by the elders obtained a good testimony.

By faith we understand that the worlds were framed by the word of God, so the things which are seen were not made by the things which are visible.

(Hebrews 11:1-3)

Dedication

In loving memory of my daughter Danielle,
we miss you.

Love always,
Dad.

About the Author

Robert C. Luisi Jr. - former captain under Joey Merlino. Originally an associate of the Patriarca crime family, he joined the Philadelphia mob and became inducted in 1998. On November 6, 1995, his father, cousin, brother and family friend were killed by gunman Anthony Clemente who fired 13 shots inside of a Charlestown restaurant. It is noted that he attempted to seize control of the criminal rackets of Whitey Bulger in Boston during the 1990s, and attempted to meet Kevin Weeks in 1998. He was indicted by the FBI on June 28, 1999, alongside 13 others for conspiracy to acquire and distribute cocaine. In 2000, he admitted to the murder of Anthony DiPrizio in 1997.

Table of Contents

Introduction

Dear Brethren,

I would like to take this opportunity to introduce myself to you. I am a theologian and have been a passionate teacher of the word of God for over a decade. And over the years I have been given the opportunity to teach to some very diverse groups of students. In each group there would always be a student who would feel the need to bestow a nickname upon me. But of all the many pseudo nicknames that were bestowed upon me over the years, "The Prophet" was the one most commonly used by my students.

Now, by allowing my students to refer to me by this nickname, "The Prophet", I am not declaring myself to be an actual prophet. Nor am I saying that I have been placed, by the Holy Spirit, into the office of prophet; although, I do believe I possess the gift of prophecy (1 Corinthians 12:9). However, it is by this gift of prophecy that I am able to reveal to you the secrets that are locked inside this book.

For the past nine or so years, I have been teaching an in-depth theology course on various specific subjects relating to creation. Many have left my classes with a deeper spiritual awareness, and still others have left as they came, criticizing and doubtful. The same will also apply to whoever decides to embark on this journey through the Bible with me. Will you open the pages of this book with an open mind and receptive heart, or will you allow your religious and worldly belief systems to be a stumbling block to you? I say this: to understand, to comprehend, you must allow the Word to uproot those old belief systems that are so deeply imbedded in your heart. Cast away those weeds of doubt and disbelief and allow the living word of God to take root in your heart and reveal His redemptive plan for your life.

Remember this one thing, that the Lord rewards those who diligently seek Him.

Creation (the belief that God was and is the Creator of all that is seen and unseen) went virtually undisputed in the Judeo-Christian orthodoxy until the 19th century.

In the year 1859, Charles Darwin, an English biologist, published his theory of evolution in a book titled "Origins of Species". Darwin's claim was that life evolved over long periods of time, basically turning the recorded creation account in the Book of Genesis into nothing more than a mythical story.

By the late 1800s, evolution was gradually becoming an academic nightmare to the many conservative Christian groups across the country. Creationism was about to be supplanted by evolution, in the minds of our children, by a theory. Darwinism was about to turn the academic world upside down and cripple the underlining belief system of Judaism and Christianity.

Today, many devout creationist and church leaders are still taking up the fight to have creationism taught in classrooms in both religious and public learning institutions. This would give our children an opportunity to make a choice between their faith and secular beliefs. Unfortunately, Evolution is still the preferred curriculum in our school systems here and abroad. Why? Tangibility. Scientists come along with their Bunsen burners, microscopes, fossils, and meteor rocks. As Christians, we come along with a Bible preaching faith. Yes, it is by faith in Christ Jesus that we believe. However, faith is not a tangible thing to those who are perishing.

I, myself, once lacked the faith in Christ Jesus, and, being taught Evolution from an early age, allowed this Darwinian Theory to take root in my heart. Being of the "baby boomer" generation and attending public schools from elementary through high school, I was taught that we as human beings evolved from a lower species of primate. I believed it. Why? No one had ever taught me anything to the contrary. Yes, my mother instilled some basic Christian fundamentals in my heart, but unfortunately not enough to contradict what I was being taught in my elementary school classroom. Those beliefs that I was taught in school, all those many years ago, stayed with me until I found my Savior in my late thirties.

So, how do we protect the children of this generation from being deceived by these secular teachings in our modern-day classrooms?

First and foremost, a child's belief system should be molded and developed in the home. It is the responsibility of the parents to train and teach their children in biblical principles before they are exposed to a worldly belief system.

Secondly, a textbook must be developed by trusted biblical scholars and theologians that will accommodate the curriculums of our public and private school systems. I am not speaking of those many children's textbooks with oversized illustrations of cartoon elephant heads poking out of the windows of Noah's ark. I am suggesting a textbook that properly timelines the Bible, from the Book of Genesis through the Book of Revelations. I have created such a curriculum for my creationism class. I am not suggesting that my curriculum is a worthy enough teaching tool for today's parents and school systems, but we do have much to consider concerning this issue.

Hosea wrote, under divine inspiration, "My people are destroyed for the lack of knowledge..." If we are without knowledge, so will our children be without knowledge, and their children, and their children's children. We, as responsible brethren of the church, must attempt to reinstate these teachings and Christian values into our school systems and into the hearts of the children of this present generation. Let us as responsible parents breathe life into this spiritually dying generation. With much love, patience, and persistence, I believe that we can reach our youth and bring them into the fold. But we must remember this one thing—education, or lack of it, begins in the home. Introduction to the Lord's Calendar of Creation:

There is a great misconception that all that was to be created has been created. However, this philosophy of completion is inaccurate. The Father has not finished with the heavens or the earth. But both, and all that are in them, are still in a transitional state, just as man is still in a transitional state. We must first put on the cloak of immortality before we can reign with our Lord in paradise.

Also, I will be exposing many date that are locked in the scriptures. Most of these dates pertain to the end of time events of Revelations' many prophecies. I do not know the date, day, or hour of Christ's return, nor am I trying to calculate any such date. No one, not even Christ, knows the date or hour of His return, but Jesus did say we would know the season (see Mt. 24:32—44). Keep this in mind through your readings: I am not predicting or trying to predict His triumphant return. Many who have attempted to calculate this unattainable date over the past centuries have failed miserably. Why? Because there is no date to be found. If the date of His return were somewhere locked in the Scripture, it would have to be revealed to us at some point in time. Our Lord said, "For everyone who asks receives, and he who seeks finds, and to him who knocks it will be open" (Lk. 11:10). Jesus also said, "If you ask anything in My name, I will do it" (Jn. 14:14). According to Scripture, if the Lord knew the date of His return, He would have to reveal it to us. This is why He specifically stated, "But of that day and hour no one knows...but Father only."

Another difficulty with trying to calculate this unattainable date is the fact that our modern-day calendar does not exactly align with the birth of Christ or the biblical timeline of the Creation story. In fact, many scholars, historians, and theologians believe that Jesus may have been born about the year 7 BC. I believe that he may have been born about the year 2 BC, I will explain the reasoning for my estimated time of His birth in future chapters.

Last week I read a short editorial in *The Week* magazine. It was titled "Bad Week for" and it discussed everyone who bought one of those "2012" books after new research found an error in the conversion of Mayan to modern calendars. This means that the "End of Days" predicted by the Mayan calendar is not December 21, 2012, but may actually be 50 to 100 years later. This excerpt was taken from "The Week" magazine, November 5, 2010 edition.

This editorial pertains to what I mentioned in the above paragraphs. It is an impossibility to calculate any such dates. This is the main reason for so many miscalculations of the end times. How can we predict the end of things if we do not know the beginning of things? We cannot, so I suggest that we stop trying.

In the year 2000, after reading the Bible front to back several times, I received a conscious vision while lying in the darkness of my bedroom. A calendar appeared hanging in the air above my bed. The odd thing about this calendar was not that it had a ghostly appearance but that it was not our normal 30-day calendar. This calendar only displayed 15 days. I began to ponder about what I had just seen, and then it came to me. This is the Lord's Calendar of Creation, meaning that in fifteen days (that is, in fifteen millennia) all things will be completed. When I woke the next morning, I began recording all the visions and revelations that I had received concerning Creation. I now began to see the sixty-six books of the Bible in a different light. All of the wisdom and knowledge that I had received pertained to the full Creation account and the biblical timeline of the 66 books.

There are many who disagree with the timeline of the Creation Calendar, especially the first six days of Creation. Throughout most of the church's history, it was believed that these first six days were actually six 24-hour days, not millennial in length. Although the advent of modern science has turned many from this 24-hour belief, the church is still unwilling to entirely abandon this tradition.

One of the first areas that the Lord begins to deal with many new believers is their lack of patience. I may have been one of His most impatient children. As soon as I began receiving these many visions and revelations of His Word, my reaction was to get this knowledge to the church. I did everything I could to get my writings to the public, but the more I tried, the harder the obstacles became. Eventually, I had come to realize that the Lord was still perfecting my teachings and dealing with my imperfections. We must realize that the Lord is very patient in all His doing. So, the question I pose to you is why would He rush to complete His creation in six 24-hour days when He has all of eternity?

Is there anywhere written in the Scriptures that God was in a rush, in a hurry? I do not think so. Isn't it written in 2 Peter 3:8 "But beloved, do not forget this one thing, that with the Lord one day is as a thousand years, and a thousand years is as one day"? And, in this verse, doesn't Peter tell us that He is long-suffering concerning us? Not impatient, but patient over long periods of time? So I ask again is God in a rush?

The fledgling church of Peter's day had no such doctrine pertaining to any six 24-hour teaching regarding Creation. The belief of the early church was that the first seven days of Creation were actually millennial days. Neither the Rabbinical Priesthood nor the Disciples of Christ were ever swayed from this belief. Nevertheless, centuries of theological opinions swayed today's modern church to a different interpretation of the scriptures. Following the crucifixion of our Lord Jesus, many doctrines, gospels, and epistles regarding His life and teachings were written by His followers and the followers of His disciples. A total of 27 of these many writings were chosen to make up the New Testament found in our modern-day Bible. For many centuries, the writings that were not chosen for the New Testament were believed to be lost to time. However, in 1945, a great discovery was made in Nag Hammadi, Egypt. A farmer was out tilling and plowing his field when he came upon an old clay pot containing more than 46 lost epistles and gospels that are believed to be written in the first and second centuries. Included in these lost texts was a copy of a forgotten treasure "The Letter of Barnabas". This non-canonical epistle was and is still believed to be the 28th book of the New Testament. But, for some unknown reason, it was not included with the 27 canonical writings. For the fact that it was not included with the original 27, I do not teach Barnabas' epistle as a biblical doctrine, but as an historical doctrine.

Chapter 15 of Barnabas' epistle is in direct relation to the beliefs of the first and second century churches regarding Creation and its origin. The following excerpt was taken from *The Lost Scriptures* by Bart D. Ehrman, pages 232-233.

1. *Something is also written about the Sabbath in the Ten Commandments, which God spoke to Moses face to face on Mount Sinai: "Make the Sabbath of the Lord holy, with pure hands and a pure heart."*

2. *In another place it says, "If my children keep the Sabbath, I will bestow My mercy on them."*

3. *This refers to the Sabbath at the beginning of Creation: "God made the works of His hands in six days, and He finished on the seventh day; and He rested on it and made it holy."*

4. *Pay attention, children, to what it means that "he finished in six days". This means that in six thousand years the Lord will complete all things. For with Him a day represents a thousand years. He Himself testifies that I am right when He says "See, a day of the Lord will be like a thousand years." And so, children, all things will be completed in six days–that is to say, in six thousand years.*

5. *"And he rested on the seventh day." This means that when His Son comes, He will put an end to the age of the lawless one, judge the impious, and alter the sun, moon, and stars; then He will indeed rest on the seventh day.*

6. *Moreover, it says, "Make it holy with pure hands and a pure heart." We are very much mistaken if we think that at the present time anyone, by having a pure heart, can make holy the day that the Lord has made holy.*

7. *And so you see that at that time, when we are given a good rest, we will make it holy–being able to do so because we ourselves have been made upright and have received the promise, when lawlessness is no more and all things have been made new by the Lord. Then we will be able to make the day holy, after we ourselves have been made holy.*

8. *Moreover He says to them, "I cannot stand your new moons and Sabbaths. You see what He means: It is not the Sabbaths of the present time that are acceptable to me, but the one I have made, in which I will give rest to all things and make a beginning of an eighth day, which is the beginning of another world."*

9. *Therefore also we celebrate the eighth day with gladness, for on it Jesus arose from the dead, and appeared, and ascended into Heaven.*

Verses 1-9 lend much credibility to my 15-day calendar of Creation. In fact, the writings align perfectly with the calendar. Since I received Ehram's book in 2003, it has been a very helpful tool in opening the eyes of my students to a new belief system. One based on the Word of God and not personal interpretations.

Let us now begin to decipher the calendar of Creation one day at a time, beginning with the first day of creation.

(Genesis 1:1–5)

THIS IS THE LORD'S 15 DAY CALENDAR OF CREATION

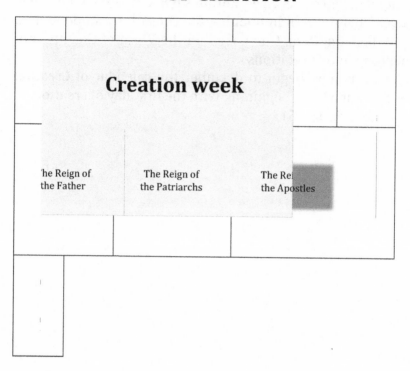

That with the Lord one day is as a thousand years,
"But, beloved, do not forget this one thing
And a thousand years is as one day..."

2 Peter 3:8

Chapter 1

The First Week of Creation:

From cover to cover of our modern-day Bible is a total of sixty-six books and epistles. During the course of this teaching, we will touch upon many of them, especially the first several chapters of Genesis, which gives us a brief summary of the creation account. However, in order to understand the beginning we must be able to comprehend the middle and the end of this recorded account of Creation. Creation begins in Genesis, but ends in the final chapters of Revelations. All things must be made new. And until that time, the earth and all that is in it will keep developing towards its final stages of purification.

Let's open these teachings with the first verses of Genesis.

The First Millennium: Gen. 1: 1—5

When the Lord came upon this universe, the earth was without form and void; and a blanket of darkness covered the heavens. So, then, we can say that the earth was here, in an uninhabitable form, before the Lord came upon it. The Word also mentions that the Lord hovered over the waters. The waters that He actually hovered over would have been in the form of ice. Today, with the sun hung in the center of the galaxy, the temperature outside the Space Station is -140° Fahrenheit. I would imagine that the temperature of the galaxy, in its chaotic stage, must have been much colder.

So, then, we can conclude that the earth was no more than a mega-asteroid, mostly composed of iron, granite, and ice. The other three inner planets—Mercury, Venus, and

Mars—are also made up of such solid materials. They all might have even been, at one time, giant fragments of a once unstable universe.

As the Lord formed this once mega-asteroid into what we call the earth today, it heated up under its immense weight and became a molten ball of rock. Now the waters began to come to the surface of the earth, rapping its sphere in a thick blanket of liquid that would begin to cool its crust. Science states that the earth is about 6 billion years old. What bothers me about this theoretical date is the fact that our still-cooling planet has a crust that is only 19 miles in thickness at its densest point and only 3 miles at its most fragile point. Do you realize, by comparison, that the shell of a common egg found in your refrigerator is both denser and thicker than our earth's crust? Fortunately for the earth and its inhabitants gravity is the key that holds this fragile and unstable planet in one piece. To me, this is just more evidence of the youthful age of today's earth.

Once the Lord had finished forming the earth He said "Let there be light", and there was light. This light was not of a star or of the sun, but of His illuminated glory. We have an example of this illumination in Revelations 21: 23. "The city had no need for the sun or the moon to shine in it. For the glory of God illuminated it. The Lamb is its light." The scriptures reveal to us that the sun, moon, and stars were not created until the fourth day of Creation.

These were the events that had occurred on the Lord's first day of Creation.

The Second Millennium: vs. 6 – 8

Then the Lord said "Let there be a firmament (sky) in the midst of the waters, and let it divide the waters from the waters."

We know that when the waters came up to the earth's surface, the waters must have resembled the water of a boiling cauldron. This would have caused the entire surface of the earth to be covered in a very thick and dense layer of moisture. Have you ever driven through a dense fog bank with only a few feet of visibility? If so, try to picture this dense cloud of moisture that hovered over the waters on the second day of Creation. I would imagine that you would be able to cut it with a knife.

Now, as the earth cooled under this thick cloud of vapor, the clouds were lifted up from the face of the waters and placed in the atmosphere. Today, the clouds remain at altitudes ranging from 6,500 to 23,000 feet above sea level. These same waters that hover in our skies today as a result of our Lord lifting them up are also the result of liquid evaporation ascending up into the heavens. However, this evaporation process has been cut nearly a hundred-fold due to the cooling of the earth's waters.

This is all that occurred on our Lord's second day of Creation.

The Third Millennium: vs. 1: 9 – 13

"Then God said 'Let the waters under the heavens be gathered together into one place [world ocean called Panthalassa], and let the dry land appear [Pangaea]"; and it was so. v. 9

Imagine what a sight this must have been when the waters of this earth began to be displaced, as the rapidly ascending ocean floor began to breach its surface. Now, when I say "rapidly", I'm not suggesting that the dry land appeared within a day, but I do believe it took no more than a century or two to completely breach the top of the waters.

There are many theories pertaining to this "dry land" that was raised up from the waters on this third day of Creation. The science community believes, as I do, that the seven continents (North and South America, Europe, Asia, Africa, Antarctica, and the island continent of Australia) were once a super-continent called Pangaea (from the Greek *pangaia*, meaning "all earth"). This single landmass remained whole until the post-flood era of Noah's descendants, (Gen. 10: 22 – 25).

Today we know that 71% of the earth's surface is covered in water, meaning that two-thirds of the earth's crust is concealed under vast oceans and seas. Nevertheless, with today's advanced technology, oceanographers and other scientists are beginning to explore ever-deeper depths of this once-hidden aquatic world. They have deduced that 57% of the crust that lies under the ocean floor is roughly about 3 miles in thickness.

If the majority of today's ocean floors are only 3 miles in thickness, and the earth is only about 13 thousand years old, based on the Lord's Calendar of Creation, I wonder about the thickness of the "dry land" that was raised up 10 thousand years ago on the third day of Creation. We, today, could only estimate the thickness, density, and stability of this giant landmass. I believe that its vast terrain, at that time, was unsettled and unpredictable. However, it was obviously stable enough to bring forth living organisms.

"Then God said, 'Let the earth bring forth grass, and the herbs that yield seed, and the fruit tree that yields fruit according to its kind, whose seed is in itself, on the earth'; and it was so." Vs. 11

We know today, by basic science and the study of botany that plant life thrives on the soil it roots in, the waters that fall from the heavens, and gases (such as carbon dioxide) which make up the atmosphere that encircles our planet. We know that plant life is the substance that sustains all living creatures that creep, crawl, walk, fly, and swim under the waters of the deep. However, on the third day of Creation, these living organisms were sowed into the earth—not only to be a future food source, but to be a living organic filtering system that would cleanse the earth's atmosphere of all deadly poisonous gases that would be harmful to our earth's inhabitants. The abundant plant life (which covered the entire continent of Pangaea) exhibits its process of photosynthesis by taking in carbon dioxide and other harmful gasses through the leaves of the plants and trees to produce gaseous oxygen

Oxygen—the breath of life for all creatures who dwell on Earth, both on land and in the seas—was beginning to replace the harmful ancient gases that polluted our skies with a life-giving aroma that was pleasing to God. The earth's ecosystem was being prepared for its next stage of evolution.

This is all that occurred on our Lord's third day of Creation.

The Fourth Millennium: vs. 14 – 19

"Then God said, 'Let there be lights in the firmament of the heavens to divide the day from the night; and let them be for signs and seasons and for days and years...'" v. 14

For three millennia the earth has been illuminated by God's glory. On this fourth day of Creation, the Father sets His sights on the heavens. He hung the sun in the center of our galaxy and the moon on the shoulders of the earth. He then formed and shaped both the inner and outer plants and fastened them to the sun.

From this time forward the sun would give its light and warmth to the earth. The plant life that was seeded on the third day of Creation, covering the entire continent of Pangaea, would now be subjected to day and night, seasons and time, climate changes, etc. The earth's plant life would now learn to adapt itself to its 365.4 days of rotation around its fledgling sun.

The scientific world would like you to believe that our sun is the source of all life on our planet. It wants us to believe that all living things that creep, crawl, walk, fly, swim, and root in the soil are the products of the sun's illumination and warmth. But here we can clearly see that all living things were not made compliments of the sun but that the sun was created to complement the earth and all its fullness.

The scientific community will never fully agree with the biblical interpretation of Creation. Nevertheless, what are written in the pages of the Bible are the hidden truths being revealed to those with understanding, who shall never perish.

Today, the sun is as essential to life on earth as the oxygen we breathe into our lungs. However, the question remains, will it continue to give its light and warmth throughout eternity?

"...He made the stars also." v. 16

What does it mean that "He made the stars also"? Astronomers have concluded that the heavenly lights (stars) that illuminated the night skies are great gaseous balls of self-illumination, hung on the outskirts of our solar system. We agree, but disagree regarding their origins.

According to the biblical record, the stars of heaven are the illumination of the angels (sons of God), who were, on this fourth day of Creation, created in His image. They were created, the sons and heirs of His heavenly kingdom. Although there is no written account of the creation of the angels and spiritual realm in the many texts of the Bible, we can still surmise much of what must have occurred on this fourth day.

The Angels

Genesis 2:7 gives us a very clear account of the creation of Adam, another speaking spirit. "Then the Lord God formed man [the flesh] from the dust of the ground and breathed into his nostril the breath or spirit of life, and man became a living being." (Amplified version)

God breathed "the spirit of life" into Adam, and he became "another speaking spirit", which means the spirits (angels) that reign in the heavenly realm were created in this same manner. They are the true essence of the life giving breath of God. And as the Father breathed each (spiritual) life into existence, He illuminated a star in the heavens according to the glory in which they were created. "...for one star [angel] differs from another star [angel] in glory." (1 Cor. 15:41)

The Father also made a comparison to the stars of His heavenly kingdom to Abraham's future descendants, whom would become as abundant and innumerable "as the sand which is on the seashore" (Gen. 22:16-19)

It is recorded in the gospel of Matthew, 2:1-12, that on the evening of Christ's birth, a star was illuminated over His birthplace in Bethlehem of Judea. Jesus, whom was brought forth as "another speaking Spirit", inspired the Father to illuminate a star in heaven, announcing to the world the birth of His son, the King of kings and the Lord of lords. Also, reference Rev. 9: 1 – 2, which again directly links the stars to the angels.

Today we look up into the night sky to see an innumerable host of stars that seem to encircle the entire outskirts of our solar system. Is our solar system, which is made up of great celestial circles such as the earth, sun, and moon, itself encased in a greater celestial circle? Is it probable that if we were to look upon our solar system from the vastness of space, that it would appear to the onlooker as one great ball of glistening lights (or even a single star) casting the light of God's Glory throughout the outer reaches of time?

I will be considering much more of the heavenly realm and the angelic beings, who were created on this fourth day, in the upcoming pages and chapters of this text.

This is all that occurred on the Lord's fourth day of Creation.

The Fifth Millennium: vs. 20 – 23

"So God created great sea creatures and every living thing that moves, with which waters abound, according to their kind, and every winged bird according to its kind. And God saw that it was good." v. 21

In the beginning of this fifth day, the waters of the deep cooled to a life-sustaining temperature and the air has been cleansed of most of its deadly poisonous gases that would be harmful to the survival of the Lord's living creatures. On this day of creation the oceans, seas, lakes, rivers, and ponds of Pangaea were teeming with life. Every gilled fish and air-breathing mammal such as the great whale, porpoise, and sea lion, shark, salmon, and guppy were all thriving and multiplying in the waters.

The skies also began teeming with every species of flying (feathered) bird, from the great eagle to the lowly canary. The question is why every bird would and feathered fowl is the first creatures to inhabit the earth? One reason might be related to this: Have you ever heard the expression, "I feel trapped like a canary in a coal mine"? About four centuries ago, the canary, an indigenous bird of the Canary Islands, was brought to Europe and was domesticated. The Europeans fancied the canary as a household pet. The canary that we see today in so many American homes was once used by the mining industry, as a warning device against toxic gases that had the parental of seeping into the mind without warning and taking the lives of miners. The lungs of the canary are very delicate and susceptible to the slightest change of the quality of air in its environment. So, the canary was taken down into the mines since the slightest amount of gas beginning to seep into the mine would affect the delicate lungs of the canary. Knowing that the canaries would succumb very quickly to these gases, the miners were hopeful that they would be given enough time to evacuate the mines.

Because of the canary's delicate lungs, many miners were spared their lives to work another day. What does all this mean in the Creation story? The canary, and many of its other small-feathered descendants that were created on this fifth day, were also used by the Father in this manner. Obviously, if the canary and many of the smaller species of bird were able to thrive in this vast ecosystem of Pangaea, the earth was ready for its next stage of evolution. The creation of the herbivore, carnivore, and omnivore.

This is all that occurred on our Lord's fifth day of Creation

The Sixth Millennium: vs. 24 – 31

"Then God said, 'Let the earth bring forth the living creature according to its kind: cattle and creeping things and beasts of the earth, each according to its own kind'; and it was so." v. 24

For nearly three thousand years, the vegetation of the earth had been abounding with no creeping thing or cattle to eat of its abundance. Some paleontologists theorized that the earth's abounding plant life in that (Jurassic) time period might have shot up a few hundred feet into the air. I agree. In today's California Redwood forest, a redwood standing 368 feet in height was discovered. This is not the only species of tree capable of reaching heights above 100 feet. Many of the great forests that are spread over our continents boast many varieties of sky-scraping giants. So, then, with no living creatures to eat of the earth's luscious green vegetation, it may have grown very high, dense, and unruly. Do you believe that the beast of the field that roams the African plains or the bison that once roamed the Great Plains of North America, were capable of consuming the vegetation of this (Jurassic) period in earth's evolution? It's highly doubtful. This was the age of the dinosaur.

Our fossil record indicates that, during this period in our earth's development, large warm- and maybe cold-blooded herbivores, carnivores, and omnivores roamed the vast continent of Pangaea. The dinosaurs who were created on this sixth day came in many different shapes and sizes. Fossil evidence shows that some of these Jurassic period creatures were only the size of the modern-day turkey. Still others were massive in size, such as *supersaurus* (an herbivore), who reached lengths of up to 120 feet. Scientist believe another dinosaur, an even larger herbivore (named ultrasaurus) also roamed the earth at this time. These were massive creatures who were believed to weigh in at nearly 80 tons. Imagine the tons of vegetation each one of these massive creatures must have consumed on a daily basis. As these massive beasts began slowly eating their way through the vast jungles, wetlands, and forests of Pangaea, very large open plains were being left in their wake. These plains that would now become host to tall grasses and edible shrubbery bearing flowers and fruit were now readying the earth to usher in its next group of herbivores, carnivores, and omnivores—the beasts of the plains.

The wildebeest, zebra, gazelle, bison, and other such creators that once roamed the great plains of Pangaea and the great plains of today's continents are the post-flood descendants of those animals on Noah's ark (Gen. 7: 6 - 12). These herbivores of today's Great Plains once strived and also thrived in great numbers alongside the T-Rex, Supersaurus, and the Ultrasaurus.

"...And God saw that it was good."

The Creation of Adam: vs. 1:26 - 27; 2:7 - 25

"Then God said, 'Let Us make man in Our image, according to Our likeness, let them have dominion over the fish of the sea, over the birds of the air, and over the cattle, over all the earth and over every creeping thing that creeps on the earth'." v. 26

To whom do you think the Lord was speaking when He said "Let Us make man in Our image"? Many believe that the "Us" whom the Lord is addressing is, in fact, the Word and the Holy Spirit. I disagree. Why? If the scriptures tell us that the stars were indeed created on the fourth day, then our Lord would in fact, be addressing His sons (angels), Michael, Gabriel, Lucifer, and their mighty legions. He, the Word, and the Holy Spirit are one. Why would the Lord make this declaration to Himself?

"And the Lord God formed man of the dust of the ground, and breathed into his nostrils the breath of life; and man became a living being [another speaking spirit] v. 27

Adam (meaning: the man or reddish in tint in Hebrew) was created in the image of God and His angels (who were also created in the image of God). He was created as the other creatures of the earth, from the dust (elements) of the ground. However, what set Adam aside from the rest of creation was not only the fact that "another speaking spirit" was breathed into his nostrils, but that when Adam's spirit was to be coupled with the spirit of a woman (in the act of intercourse) their offspring would also come forth as speaking spirits. The man, Adam, was created as an angel, bound to a terrestrial body. Adam's fleshy tent wasn't just able to bring forth a twofold being, as the animals, but a threefold being of spirit, soul, and body (see 2 Tim. 5: 23). Adam's offspring were to be brought forth as sons of God, the children of the Most High. Adam was created incorruptible, and immortality was in his hands, for he was the first son of God to reign in the flesh. "...Adam, the son of God." (Lk 3: 38)

The Garden of Eden: vs. 8 - 25

Now the Father planted a garden east of Eden and placed the man there. In the garden grew every tree that bore fruit and other things. Also planted in the garden was the Tree of Life, which was the source of Adam's immortality. The leaves of the Tree were for healing, and its fruit contained a hidden enzyme that kept Adam's flesh from any form of corruption. As long as Adam ate from this Tree his flesh would never age or see decay.

Now I mustn't forget the most controversial and infamous tree that was planted in the midst of the garden: the tree of the knowledge of good and evil. Both Adam and Eve were told purposely by the father not to eat the fruit of this tree. Why? We'll have to address this controversial subject in the following chapter.

Adam names the animals: vs. 19 - 20

"So Adam gave names to all cattle, to the birds of the air, and to every beast of the field..." v. 20

God created every living creature that dwells on, in, and under the earth, but it was His son, Adam, who named them. What does it mean that God created every beast of the field and brought them to Adam, and Adam gave each of them name? We see in the creation account of chapter 1: 24 -25 that God created all the beasts of the field before He created Adam–, which he did. The dinosaurs and, most likely, the zebra, lion, bear, and bison were created before Adam.

Many scholars and theologians believe that chapter 2 of Genesis is actually a second creation story. No, it's not another interpretation of the creation story but a brief summary of the sixth day, amplifying vv.1:24 through 2: 4. The question here is did God continue to create these living creatures and beasts of the field after He created Adam? Yes. He did continue and is still creating to this day, although today most of His creations come through man.

When we read these accounts of Adam, we must remember Adam was created as a son of God. He was created as a highly intellectual being, who would often stroll through the Garden "in the cool of the day" accompanied by the Father, learning all his Father's hidden secrets concerning His creation. Adam gained knowledge of all things seen and unseen. The only knowledge that was kept from him on this sixth day of creation was his carnal nature. This is what was hidden in the forbidden fruit of the tree of knowledge which both he and Eve were commanded, by God, not to eat from.

Adam was a masterful student of the Master of all teachers, God Himself. Amen.

If we would consider Adam from his scriptural depiction, we would believe him to be nothing more than a common farmer, wielding a hoe and dressed in animal skins. But, I tell you, he was, and maybe still is, one of the most intellectual minds that have ever graced this planet, evidence of which you will learn as we follow the scriptures.

The creation of Eve: vs. 21 - 25

The Father caused a deep sleep to fall over Adam. As he slept, the Father removed one of his ribs. And from that one rib, He, the Father, created woman (Eve). When the Father brought Adam's companion back to him, he named her woman, "because she was taken out of a Man". v. 23

I believe that this verse answers that age-old question, "What came first–the chicken or the egg?" In this biblical account, man came before woman. I would also think that all the animal kingdom was brought forth in the same manner. First, the Lord created the lion and then, from his DNA, created the lioness. In this same manner, He brought forth all the living creatures that dwell on the earth. And why was the female created for the male? Procreation– to bring forth another generation of the flesh, with each to its own kind. So, the Lord created the rooster and, seeing that it was good, created the hen from the rooster's DNA, and the hen brought forth the egg. What does all this mean? The chicken came before the egg.

"And the man and his wife were both naked and were not embarrassed or ashamed in each other's presence." Amp. 2:25)

What does it mean that they were neither "embarrassed nor ashamed in their nakedness"? Were they naked 24/7? Or was the writer trying to stress to the reader their innocence concerning their carnal nature?

In our present day society, the majority of both men and women dress very modestly, but still others dress very provocatively. Why so much variation in our society's present-day dress codes? Can it be a moral issue? A personal issue? A sexual issue? On the other hand, maybe the causes of our dress codes are an instinctual behavioral issue for attracting the opposite sex. I would have to say all of the above, and more. In the case of Adam and Eve, it was not a question of provocation or promiscuity concerning their clothing, or the lack thereof, but a natural state of existence. Adam and Eve both were naive concerning the secondary (sensual) use of the genitalia (procreation). Therefore, lacking the knowledge of their carnal nature, they did not consider themselves naked.

In the summer months many of us venture to the many beaches and lakes of this great country. The first thing we notice is both men and women are scarcely clad in tiny bikinis and swimsuits, exposing, in many cases, more than 90% of their bodies. I ask do we consider these scarcely clad bodies to be naked. No. Why? Because their genitalia is covered. As provocative as some may believe these beach goers are dressed, they're still not considered naked.

Another observation concerning the nakedness of Adam and Eve (mentioned in verse 25) is not to misinterpret the writer's symbolic meaning of their unclad bodies. The writer was expressing their innocence regarding their carnal nature, not that they literally pranced about the garden naked every day. That would be very unlikely considering the possible region of Pangaea that we believe to be "the cradle of life", called Mesopotamia (from the Greek "land between the rivers"—meaning the Tigris and Euphrates rivers located in modern day Iraq).

Iraq lies between 30 degrees and 32 degrees north latitudes. The climate of the Tigris-Euphrates Basin, believed to be the biblical Eden, is overwhelmingly hot in the summer months (reaching temperatures ranging between 100 and 120 degrees Fahrenheit and is very humid near the rivers). During winter months, the temperatures drop to about 60 to 75 degrees during the day and just above freezing temperature at nighttime.

It seems that the present-day Iraq would have been an ideal place for the Lord to plant His garden, eastward of Eden. However, the problem with today's Iraq is that it does not share the same northern latitudes of the biblical Eden. Remember, on the sixth day of Creation, the earth was still one big mass. I estimate, through my studies, that at least 80 to 85% of Pangaea's landmass sat above the Equator. This would mean that today's Iraq may have sat somewhere between 60 to 70 degrees northern latitudes and 0 to 30 degrees eastern longitude in the vicinity of modern-day Sweden and Finland.

Both Sweden and Finland boast a much cooler climate than Iraq. Nevertheless, both northern countries host a large variety of plant life and dense forest, with temperatures ranging in the high 80s. At these latitudes, the biblical Garden of Eden would have had no problems hosting a variety of plant life and a host of fruit-bearing trees. Eden, even at this latitude, would be able to provide a "clothes-optional" climate in the summer season.

The name given to the first man, Adam, has a dual meaning in the Hebrew tongue. The first meaning is "the man" and the second meaning is "of reddish tint" or "ruddy-looking". Ruddy or reddish tint would describe Adam's facial complexion as being white and capable of blushing. Adam's skin pigment also suggests to me that he was created in a cooler climate.

This completed the Lord's sixth day of creation.

"Thus the heavens and the earth, and all the host of them, were finished." And then "He [the Father] rested."

Chapter 2

The Sabbath Rest: vs. 3: 1 – 7

"Then God blessed the seventh day and sanctified it, because in it He rested from all His work which God had created and made." v. 2: 3

Our Lord rested on the Sabbath day, leaving the heavenly (spiritual) realm under the authority of His three chief princes—Michael (whose name means "who is like God"), Gabriel (whose name means "hero of God"), and Lucifer (whose name means "light bearer"). Michael, who seemed to be the most revered of the three, is revealed by Daniel to be one of the chief princes in chapter 10: 13 ("The great prince who stands watch over the sons of your people [Israel]"). In chapter 12:1 of the New Testament, Jude vs. 9 also applies the title of archangel to Michael. The term archangel means: a chief or principle angel.

Gabriel, who declared in the gospel of Luke, "I am Gabriel, who stands in the presence of God..." (Luke 1:19). Gabriel was sent to Zacharias to announce the birth of his son, John, who would be later known as John the Baptist. Gabriel also announced to Mary the conception of her son Jesus (vs. 26 – 38). It is also recorded in Daniel 8: 16 and 9: 21 of Gabriel being sent to Daniel by God to interpret Daniel's many visions regarding the tribulations of his people, the Israelites.

However, neither in the Old nor New Testaments, nor the many Apocryphal writings, are any other angelic beings given the title of archangel or chief prince.

The angel Raphael, whose name means "God has healed", revealed himself as "...one of seven angels who enter and serve before the Glory of God" in the book of Tobit (12:15). The seven who were spoken about by Raphael in the book of Tobit are recorded in the first book of Enoch (both the books of Tobit and of Enoch are Apocryphal writings).

The Book of Enoch mentions Michael, Gabriel, and Raphael, along with four other angels (Uriel, Raguel, Sariel, and Remiel) as "...the seven angels who enter and serve before the Glory of God". These five angels who are included with Michael and Gabriel may be princes of the heavenly realm who enter into the presence of God. However, being chief princes or archangels seems very questionable to me. In all the 66 books (canonical writings) of the Bible, Michael is the only angelic being given the title of archangel. He, Michael, is the principle angel of the heavenly realm and, along with Gabriel and Lucifer, reigned over the angelic beings that were created on the fourth day. The heavens host an innumerable amount of princes, such as Raphael and Uriel, and under these principalities sits many powerful and high-ranking angels. These are the lords and overlords who control the legions governed by generals, captains of hundreds (centurions), captains of fifty, captains of tens, lieutenants, corporals, sergeants, and foot soldiers. Many of these legions, if not all, retained regiments of the mighty cherubim (two-winged angels) and the powerful sentry angels, called seraphim (six-winged angels). These princes and legions, who were placed under the authority of the three chief princes, were to reign in peace during the Father's Sabbath (millennial) rest. But as in every reigning kingdom, empire, principality, etc., that has ever ruled during the history of creation, the Father's heavenly kingdom was about to suffer treason, treachery, and sedition. One of the heavenly realm's chief princes was about to rebel, he and his legions, against the precepts set forth by his heavenly Monarch, God Himself.

"How you have fallen from heaven, O Lucifer [morning star], son of the morning! How you are cut to the ground, you who weakened the nations!" (Isa. 14:12).

Lucifer, who also held the titles of "son of the morning" and "covering cherub", is recorded in both the books of Isaiah and Ezekiel. In each recorded account, he is betrayed as a perverse adversary of the Most high. How did this once "covering cherub", who reigned as one of the chief princes of the heavenly realm, fall to such a state of degradation and contempt?

The answer to this question may lie in the attributes that were granted to him on the day he was created. His most gifted attributes are recorded in Ezekiel 28: "You were the seal of perfection; full of wisdom and perfect in beauty...You were perfect in all your ways from the day you were created" (vv. 12, 14 – 15).

Perfection, wisdom, and beauty were Lucifer's distinguishing qualities that set him apart from all the other angelic beings. It is also recorded in verse 13 that his instruments, with their settings, sockets, and engravings (timbrels and pipes) were wrought from pure gold and prepared for him on the day he was created. This means that he was created as a masterful player and conductor of every wind, string, and percussion instrument of the heavens above. His ear was attuned to every instrumental and lyrical note that graced the heavens. He was truly the personification of perfection in every aspect of his being.

However, these same attributes of perfection would become the cause of this once great and mighty cherub and prince of the heavenly realm to topple and fall. Lucifer's fall and crash was so great that today we consider him to be no more than a scurrilous scoundrel and enemy of humankind.

"Vanity of vanities"

As the Father's Sabbath Day of rest continued on, Lucifer grew exceedingly confident and self-absorbed in his own passions. Casting aside the precepts of his Father, he began to govern over his legions with an unrestrained passion for self-fulfillment. His wisdom and beauty were so alluring to the so many angelic beings under his authority that he easily seduced and manipulated them in both a physical and intellectual manner. Lucifer's homoerotic behavior quickly spread through the ranks of his legions, causing nearly one third of the spiritual realm to fall to lewd and lascivious behaviors that would ultimately cause iniquity to reign in the loins of the angels.

The reason I refer to Lucifer's sexually deviant behavior as "homoerotic" is the fact that the angelic beings were not created male and female (as Adam and Eve were) but were, in fact, all the same sex (male). The angels were not created as Adam was to have heirs by procreation. Yes, the angelic beings had knowledge of their celestial anatomies and the fact that they were capable of having sexual intercourse. However, they also knew that the same laws that were to govern the physical realm concerning sexual conduct (terrestrial bodies) also applied to the spiritual realm (celestial bodies). "You shall not lie with a male as with a female. It is an abomination...Do you not know that...neither fornicators, nor idolaters, nor homosexuals, nor sodomites...will inherit the kingdom of God" (Lev. 18:22 and 1 Cor. 6: 9 – 10).

Chaos now ruled supremely over Lucifer's domain, as angel lusted after angel, doing what is considered abominable in the sight of God. Lucifer, who was clothed in a garment of precious stones from the day he was created (Ez. 28:13), was now covered in the filth of his disobedience.

I'm sure that there were many angels under the authority of Lucifer who defected, not willing to transgress the precepts of God, to the legions of Michael and Gabriel. The question remaining is if any of their (Michael or Gabriel's) princes, lords, or foot soldiers defected to Lucifer.

Many ask why Michael, being archangel, allowed this rebellion to take place among Lucifer's ranks. The answer to this often-asked question is free will. Lucifer and his legions exercised our Lord's most freely given gift. Free will is the path to either salvation or perdition, which Lucifer and his legions shortly were about to find out. All Michael and his legions could do was stand their ground and watch.

"The Serpent"

"Now the serpent was more cunning than any beast of the field which the Lord made..."

(Gen. 3:1).

Lucifer, being no longer content in his longing for celestial bodies of the angels, set his eye on the physical realm. He now lusted for the flesh of both Adam and his wife. Many have tried to preach over the centuries that the angels were jealous of God's creation of man and His relationship with Adam. This, I tell you, is unscriptural. Neither Lucifer nor the other angelic beings were jealous of Adam, but they became wanton for his flesh and the flesh of the woman.

Lucifer's motives for entering the garden were not inspired by jealousy, but by his unrestrained passion for the carnal flesh. Eve's forbidden fruit was so enticing to Lucifer that he entered the serpent undetected by Adam. Adam, had he known of Lucifer's scheme, could have easily rebuked him and cast him from the garden. Remember, Adam reigned on the seventh day over the earthly realm, as the "Lord of the Sabbath". Lucifer had no authority over Adam or the earthly realm on this seventh day of Creation.

It doesn't seem quite logical that the serpent spoken of in Genesis chapter 3 is in fact an actual creeping or crawling reptile. However, a similar event is recorded in the book of Numbers, chapter 22.

There was a time after Israel's exodus from Egypt that they wandered upon the plains of Moab and camped there. Balak, king of the Moabites, feared the children of Israel because of their numbers and also because of knowledge of the quick victories that Israel had had over Sihon, king of the Amorites, and Og, king of the Bashanites. Balak sent his messengers to Balaam, the prophet and diviner, so that he may curse the children of Israel, saying "Therefore please come at once, curse this people for me, for they are too mighty for me..." (v. 6). So, Balaam consulted the Lord concerning this matter: "and God said to Balaam, 'You shall not go with them; you shall not curse the people [Israel], for they are blessed'" (v. 12). Balaam heeded the words of the Lord and sent Balak's messengers back to their country. Balak, still fearing the children of Israel, sent his messengers back to Balaam, this time trying to entice him with the promises of riches. The next morning, after consulting the Lord, Balaam awoke, saddled his donkey, and went off with the king's messengers to Moab. As Balaam traveled the road to Moab, accompanied by two of his servants, the donkey, seeing the path before him being blocked by an angel, crushed Balaam's foot up against a wall trying to avoid the angel. Three times the donkey tried to avoid the angel and each time Balaam struck her.

"Then the Lord opened the mouth of the donkey, and she said to Balaam: 'What have I done to you that you have struck me three times?' And Balaam said to the donkey, 'Because you have abused me. I wish there was a sword in my hand, for now I would kill you!' So the donkey said to Balaam, 'Am I not the donkey which you have ridden, ever since I became yours, to this day? Was I ever disposed to do this to you?' And he said 'No'. Then the Lord opened Balaam's eyes and he saw the angel of the

Lord standing in the way with His drawn sword in His hand; and he bowed his head and fell flat on his face" (vv. 28 – 31).

There are three facts that we can gleam from this account of Balaam and his donkey. Firstly, by this account, we can clearly see that an angel (spirit) has the ability to enter and open the mouth of an animal. Secondly, that a dumb donkey was able to see the angel, whereas Balaam lacked the capability. Thirdly, Balaam's eyes were not open until the donkey spoke.

So, then, it is probable that the serpent was indeed a reptile of some sort and Lucifer was fully capable of both entering and opening the mouth of this serpent and speaking through it.

The Seduction

"...And he [Lucifer] said to the woman 'Has God indeed said 'You shall not eat of every tree of the garden'?' And the woman said to the serpent 'We may eat the fruit of the trees of the garden, but of the fruit of the tree which is in the midst of the garden, God has said 'You shall not eat of it, nor shall you touch it, lest you die'" (Gen. 3:1 – 3).

I'm sure that Lucifer's approach to seducing the woman was obviously premeditated and very calculated. He must have exercised a great deal of restraint, patience, and cunning not to cause the woman to alert Adam of his presence in the garden. I don't believe, nor do I want you to believe, that this seduction was quick and unchallenging for the serpent. We must keep in mind, according to the scriptures, that this seventh day was indeed a thousand years. It's very possible that even as cunning as Lucifer was, and is still known to be, that the woman did not quickly succumb to his tactical advances. And, again, we must remember that the woman was not a naïve, back hill, country bumpkin, but a child of the Most High.

As Lucifer lulled his victim into a state of false assurance, I'm sure he began to reveal his true identity to her, knowing that she wouldn't betray his trust and tell her husband of what had been taking place right under his nose. I believe that this was one of his main tactics in his seduction plan for the woman. It's written that he was the seal of perfection and perfect in beauty. I'm sure that his God-given attributes might have further enticed the woman to eat of the forbidden fruit. Isn't it written that "the woman saw that the tree was good for food, that it was pleasant to the eyes...?" (Gen. 3: 6). Maybe she found Lucifer to also be pleasing to the eyes.

To relate to this infamous tale of seduction, we must consider our own life experiences concerning this same type of issue. How many of you women (and also many of you men) have faced this type of sexual aggression in your lifetime? How many women out there have been relentlessly pursued by their bosses or a persistent colleague? Who knows, maybe some of you men fell prey to a wanton secretary. Maybe it was the next-door neighbor's wife or husband, or maybe a close friend of the family, who charmed you into his or her awaiting arms.

Many times in the past I have found myself on both sides of this ever-reoccurring issue, either being seduced or finding myself in the role of the seducer. In my former profession, seduction, persuasion, and manipulation were some of the tools of my trade that I most heavily relied on. How could I manipulate, either mentally or physically, what I cannot seduce? If I cannot persuade then how can I control? And if I could not control, then how can I lead? Manipulation was the key that opened all those doors that were once closed off to me. And even at the top of my (manipulation) game, most of my conquest did not succumb as quickly to my tactics as I would have liked. Many, depending on the circumstances, took months and even some years to succumb to my flatteries and persuasive tactics...as I believe it may have taken Lucifer to actually persuade the woman to eat of the tree.

Patience. Lucifer practiced patience, and, over the course of time, the woman fell to his alluring seductions. Remember, before the kiss comes the flattery. Before the flattery comes the friendship, the lust of the eyes. So then, we can say that lust of the eye is the catalyst that entices the first kiss. And what follows that first kiss, especially in the woman Eve's case, is spiritual death. How many of us have fallen in a similar manner?

"...You will not surely die...eat of it and your eyes will be open...you will be like God, knowing good and evil...she took of its fruit and ate..." (vv. 4 – 6).

With the woman taking of the tree and eating, Lucifer's conquest was nearing its completion. His patience was finally about to pay off. This once forbidden and unattainable fruit was finally in his grasp, the carnal flesh.

It is recorded in the "Zohar" (the sacred and mystical writings of the Jewish Cabalists) that Samael (Lucifer) had had intercourse with the woman in the garden, and she conceived Cain (Zohar vol. 1, pg. 448, para. 464 – 465; pg. 440, para. 455). It is also written in the pages of vol. 2 of the Zohar that the serpent injected his impurity into Eve and she became pregnant by it (pg. 203, para. 332). It is my belief that Lucifer had intercourse with the woman over long periods of time but she did not conceive during this time. Why? God had not yet visited her, which, in conjunction with the example of Sarah (the wife of Abraham), it was not yet the time for the woman to bring forth offspring (Gen. 21: 1 – 3).

Once the physical seduction of the woman was very well on its way and Lucifer began calming his lust for her, he sent the woman to Adam, hoping she would seduce him as Lucifer had seduced her.

"...She also gave to her husband with her, and he ate. Then the eyes of both of them were open, and they knew that they were naked..." (vv. 6 – 7).

Again, we see here in verses 6 – 7 that Lucifer did not go to Adam to seduce him, but sent the woman. Needless to say, Adam fell to her seduction and ate of the fruit. Now, with his eyes being open to his newly found carnal nature, he also began defiling himself with the woman, the serpent, and the angels of Heaven.

The Zohar also makes reference to Adam's sexual exploits in the garden, concerning the serpent, the woman, and the angels. "Adam clove to the unclean spirit, THE SERPENT, and his wife, Eve, clung to it first and took and received defilement from it" (vol. 2, pg. 203, para. 331)

"Two female spirits used to come and mate with him (Adam). And he bore from them spirits and demons that roam around the world" (vol. 2, pgs. 211 – 216, para. 346 – 357).

I believe, through revelations, like the Cabalists, that both Adam and his wife had intercourse with Lucifer and his angels. However, I do not agree with the mystic Zohar's sometimes-erroneous interpretations.

For example, Lucifer did enter the garden and entered into the serpent to physically seduce the woman. He then sent the woman to her husband. Once the woman persuaded Adam to eat from the tree, Lucifer revealed himself to them and began to teach them of his carnal nature. But despite all the sexual misconduct that had taken place in the garden, no child or offspring was sired.

Another example of a misinterpretation by the Zohar deals with the supposed female spirits that came to Adam. The Lord God did not create female spirits, so the fact that these two spirits are female is actually impossibility.

Nevertheless, there are today spirits who come to the sons and daughters of men and seduce them in the night. As many of us sleep, spirits of perversion may come upon us. The names given to these spirits are Incubus and Succubus. One is believed to be a female spirit preying on men; the other, a male spirit preying on women. But, I tell you, they are both one in nature. Adam slept with these male spirits as did the woman.

"Adam clove to the unclean spirit, THE SERPENT, and his wife..." This indicates that Adam allowed the iniquity and sin of sexual immorality (homosexuality and sodomy) to defile both his spirit and carnal flesh, passing down his iniquities to his coming generations. This caused death to now reign in the physical realm.

The Father's millennial rest was nearing its end, and the first week of Creation was coming to a close. One third of the heavenly beings had defiled themselves in sexual immoralities. Both Adam and Eve were about to pollute their children and the generations to come with the filth of iniquity and sin. And the cause of all this rebelliousness and deviant behavior was the act of one heavenly prince, whose insanity would cause both the heavens and the earth to be turned upside down.

Thus ended our Lord's first week of creation.

Chapter 3

The Anticipated Return:

On the dawning of this eighth day of Creation, the Most High returned to the heavenly realm and gathered the entire heavenly host (angels) to Him. As the sons of God assembled together the Father could not help but notice that Lucifer was not in the presence of the congregation. Neither his princes, lords, nor legions could be found amongst the children of the Most High. As Michael and Gabriel stood in the presence of the Father, they brought no accusations against Lucifer or his legions. However, as the Most High began to inquire into the reason for Lucifer's absence, Michael, being archangel, spoke in the presence of the assembly, saying "My Lord, Your great prince, Lucifer, has transgressed upon Your precepts and fallen into a state of sedition. He also persuaded one third of the heavenly host to follow him in his lewd and lascivious behaviors." Upon hearing Michael's words, the Lord exclaimed, "Summon Lucifer to Me!"

Lucifer Condemned to Darkness:

"O Lucifer, how you have fallen in the presence of the assembly, in the midst of My congregation. You have lifted your heart up against me, and now your fall shall be great. My light shall no longer be found in you, and in darkness you shall go. Your wisdom has been corrupted and your garment defiled in the iniquities of your pride. You shall forever be clothed in darkness and you shall reign with a scepter-forged form the scales of your conspirator. Your kingdom shall be illuminated in perpetual darkness, and no longer shall you walk among the congregation as a prince, but as an adversary [Satan].Your subjects shall be an abomination to all who share in My light. The pit (Shoel/Hades) shall be your domain, and the earth your conquest."

The Prince of Darkness:

This once "Covering Cherub" would now go by a slew of names more befitting his crimes, such as: Satan (the primary name, from the Hebrew meaning "adversary"), Devil (from the Greek *diabolos*, meaning "slanderer"), Beelzebub (from the Hebrew meaning "Lord of the Flies"), Evil One, The Dragon, The Serpent of Old, and host of others.

Satan was now the lord of the underworld and the chief adversary of the Most High. And when he was cast down from the heavenly realm, one third of the heavenly host was cast down with him. These are the demonic creatures who possess and oppress the sons of man to this day. Many of these fallen angels roam through the earth looking to devour any and all those who dwell on the earth. Still others are imprisoned under the darkness of Hades.

"And the angels who did not keep their proper domain, but left their own abode [heavenly realm], He has reserved in everlasting chains under darkness for the judgment of the great day" (Jude 6).

These many legions that are imprisoned in Hades can travel back and forth between the earthly realm and the realm of the dead. However, many need a host to dwell in the earthly realm, such as "Legions", who possessed the man from the city of Gadarenes (see Mk. 5:1-19), and without a host they are forced to return to the underworld. These minions of Satan are cursed to be as parasites until the Day of Judgment. Still, those demons who roam the earth are very powerful and well organized. We must be reminded that these demonic beings were once high-ranking angels in the kingdom of God. Some were princes, lords, and captains, who ruled over legions of foot soldiers and winged cherub and seraphim.

In Ephesians 2:2, Paul refers to Satan as "the prince of the power of the air [winged demon], the spirit who now works in the sons of disobedience". Also in Ephesians 6, he warns us of the imminent threat and authority of our spiritual enemies. "For we do not wrestle against flesh and blood, but against principalities, against powers, against the rulers of the darkness of this age, against spiritual host of wickedness in the heavenly places" (v. 12).

We must never forget the power and the spiritual authority of the enemy, for their numbers are great and their contempt for God and His precepts dictate their very actions of aggression against us—the children of Light. There is still much to write about our spiritual adversary, Satan, and his minions in these upcoming chapters. But first let us return to the matters at hand—the Lord's descent into the Garden of Eden.

Paradise Lost:

It was customary of the Father, before his millennial rest, to visit the Garden and walk with Adam in the cool of the day. On this day, however, Adam and the woman were not expecting a visit from the Father, believing He was still resting from all His work. So, they carried on in their self-indulgences, as they had done since eating the forbidden fruit. Suddenly, though, they heard the Father's footsteps in the Garden.

"Adam and his wife hid themselves from the presence of the Lord God among the trees of the Garden. Then the Lord God called to Adam and said 'Where are you?' So, he said 'I heard your voice in the Garden, and I was afraid because I was naked; and I hid myself'" (vv. 8 – 10).

So, they hid, as do we when we have done wrong. Adam and his wife were both ashamed of the carnal acts they had committed and were reluctant to reveal themselves to the Lord. It is very possible that they were in a carnal way with one another as the Father was descending into the Garden. The Father, now knowing of their disobedience, asked two very direct questions: "who told you that you were naked?" and "Have you eaten from the tree of which I commanded you that you should not?" (v. 11).

Some debate among themselves "If the Father is all-knowing, then why would He ask such obvious questions?" I've come to learn through my years of study that when the Father poses any type of question in the scriptures, such as these two questions to Adam, it is for our benefit. Any scholar or even layperson can tell you that there is a plethora of information hidden in the most obvious of questions. The question "Who told you?" reveals to me that both Adam and the woman obtained their knowledge audibly, and not through any of the other five senses. Another bit of information that can be gleamed from this particular question is this: that knowledge, in itself, is not sinful. This is why the Father posed the second question: "have you eaten from the tree?"

If I was to reveal to you, in this chapter, a fragment of knowledge hidden to you from the beginning of time that could lead you to sin, have I caused sin to enter you? NO. Knowledge, whether it pertains to good or evil, is not sinful and is not harmful unless we transgressed upon it. Adam, knowing of his now nakedness, did not allow sin to enter him. Sin entered Adam because he transgressed upon that knowledge he had gained from the serpent of his carnal nature. His lascivious behaviors with Lucifer, the angels, and the woman is what caused sin to take root in his flesh and iniquity to reign in his spirit.

The Tree of the Knowledge of Good and Evil:

The woman said to the serpent, "But of the fruit of the tree which is in the midst of the garden, God has said 'You shall not eat it, nor shall you touch it, lest you die'" (vs. 3). Do not touch, do not eat, and as soon as she transgressed these two commandments, she allowed the seeds of sin to be planted in her flesh, and her iniquities to rule over her heart (spirit).

Now then, besides the woman's act of disobedience by touching and eating the forbidden fruit (causing sin to enter her), what further harm could this fruit bring to the flesh if not instant death? If we now find it more plausible—or should I say, factual—that both Adam and the woman gained their knowledge by the spoken words of the serpent, then what was actually gained by the eating of the fruit? What were the hidden properties of this unique fruit that would cause the flesh to awaken to such carnal awareness? Perhaps it had some of the chemical properties of the cocoa leaf, bringing an arousing stimulation to the flesh, or maybe it held the pharmaceutical effects of the drug known as "Ecstasy", bringing both conscious and flesh into a state of euphoria. Whatever its properties, the flesh was now in a state of wanton fulfillment. The tree, and the fruit that it produced, was obviously unique in its nature, one of a kind, and, unlike the other fruit-bearing trees of the Garden, this tree only had one main purpose--to bring awareness to man's conscious concerning his physical (fleshy) being. Remember, man was created a three-part being: spirit, soul, and body. Until that dreadful day when the woman put the forbidden fruit to her lips, the spirit man reigned supreme over the soul and body. No conflict or schism had ever risen in the flesh prior to the woman eating the forbidden fruit. Now awakened, her flesh can only be likened to a bear just coming out of its state of hibernation, roaming about, looking to consume anything that it comes across on its path of carnage. Such is the flesh of man, once awakened. We are always working to quench the insatiable thirst and never-ending cravings of the flesh, especially for the forbidden. This is why, today, we are constantly looking for that quick fix—a new high, a new sexual experience, a new food or drink—a quick solution for a never-ending craving. We eat but our hunger is never satisfied. We drink but our thirst is never quenched. We fornicate but our desires are never fulfilled. The more we consume, the more we want, and, eventually, our wants turn to sin, and our sins lead us to death.

The flesh is only mindful of itself and host of an array of unsightly poisons that we call sin. Once the seed of sin is planted in the flesh, our consuming habits for the forbidden nourishes the seedling, allowing it to take root and sprout up. Once matured, it bears the fruits of death.

"Then the man said 'The woman whom You gave to me, she gave me of the tree, and I ate'" (v. 12).

I guess the chivalrous qualities of the medieval knighthood did not derive from our father Adam. He did not hesitate to place the blame on the woman. Neither did the woman waste any time giving up the serpent, as you can see in the following scripture:

"...the serpent deceived me and I ate" (v. 13).

Once hearing the confessions of Adam and the woman, the Lord proceeded to curse the serpent (vv. 14 – 15), and to bring condemning sentences against the woman (v. 16) and Adam (vv. 17 – 19).

<u>Adam Expelled from the Garden</u>:

"Then the Lord God said, 'Behold, the man has become like one of Us, to know good and evil. And now, least he put out his hand and take also of the tree of life, and eat, and live forever'" (v. 22)

So the Lord drove out Adam and his wife Eve from the Garden. Clothed in animal skin, man made his appearance from the Garden of God. And by the sweat of his brow, Adam tilled the ground in patience until it brought forth its life-giving fruits. Adam and Eve would never be allowed to enter into the Garden of God again. "...And He placed cherubim at the east of the Garden of Eden, and a flaming sword which turned every way to guard the way to the Tree of Life" (vs. 24). With access denied to take from the Tree of Life, Adam and Eve would now lose their immortality, and their flesh could now fall to corruption. Adam was now a common man, the first man.

Chapter 4

The Genealogy of Adam:

Soon after being expelled from the Garden, Eve gave birth to Adam's first son, Cain. Cain would become a tiller of the ground, a farmer and husbandman. The second son born to Adam was Abel, who would grow to become a keeper of livestock, a shepherd of sheep and goats. Eve also bore many daughters to Adam who would eventually be given to their brothers in marriage.

Sibling marriages were common practice in biblical times. An example of this sibling union occurred between Abraham, our father of faith, and his half-sister Sarah. Terah, the father of Abraham, was also the father of Sarah. Even though Terah fathered both children, they came from different mothers, which means that Sarah's mother may have been either one of Terah's other wives or concubines. Abraham explains this sibling union to King Abimelch in Genesis chapter 20. "But indeed she is truly my sister. She is the daughter of my father, but not the daughter of my mother; and she became my wife" (v. 12).

Incestuous marriages and affairs were commonly practiced before the law was given on Mount Sinai. Until that time, and even after the law, incest would plague the records of the Bible. We can find another example of incestuous lust between two of David's children. Amnon's lust for his half-sister Tamar resulted in rape and murder. Brother raising up against brother (see 2 Sam. 13)

Today, this practice is frowned upon in modern societies. However, incestuous marriages between first and second cousins are still practiced in most third world countries. In fact, it's welcomed.

The First Death:

Cain, being the first-born son of Adam, would be heir to all of Adam's possessions at the time of his death. Included in this right of the first-born son, Cain would also inherit the right of lineage, which meant that it would be Cain's descendants who would carry the blessing of God through their generations. Messiah would have also come through Cain's lineage if he had not risen up and killed his brother Abel.

This first act of violence is recorded in genesis chapter 4. Cain rose up and murdered his brother in the field, and although I'm certain he made some attempt to cover up his wrongdoing, it was to no avail. Once man's blood is shed in violence, the Lord will demand a reckoning for that individual's blood (Ref. Gen. 9:5 – 6). The life of all God's creatures is in the blood, it is the blood that speaks when the flesh has been slain, not the spirit.

As soon as Abel's blood cried out to the Lord, the Father quickly came upon Cain, saying, "...Where is Abel your brother?" And Cain retorted, "I do not know. Am I my brother's keeper?" And the Lord said to Cain: "What have you done? The voice of your brother's blood cries out to Me from the ground." You see it was the blood that cried out to the Lord, not the spirit. So the question that remains is: Where, then, is Abel's spirit? If the Lord did not pose this direct question to Cain—"Where is Abel your brother?"—we would have assumed, because of modern church beliefs that Abel's spirit was abiding in the heavenly realm with the Father. Unfortunately for Abel, and the rest of humankind to follow, that would not be the case. So, then, where did Abel's spirit go when he was murdered?

The spirit of man was not created to dwell in the heavenly realm, nor was his flesh ever to see corruption. Death itself had no dominion over the earthly realm until Eve placed the forbidden fruit to her mouth and ate. It was from that point on that Death became an unrelenting adversary to anyone who was born in the flesh.

Iniquity is a defilement of the spirit and sin—the defilement of the flesh. However, it is the iniquity that reigns in our heart that keeps us from communing with God. Iniquity and sin are a curse to all those who transgress God's law. This was the reason for the exile of Lucifer and his legions from the heavenly realm. These former sons of the Most High defiled themselves in their lewd behaviors causing iniquity to realm in their spiritual loins. "You were perfect in your ways [Lucifer] from the day you were created, till iniquity was found in you" (Ek. 28:15). It was not sin that reigned in the angelic beings, but iniquity.

This is what is said about iniquity in the Ten Commandments: "For I, the Lord your God, am a jealous God, visiting the iniquity of the fathers upon the children to the third and fourth generations of those who hate Me" (Ex. 20:5). This meant that the iniquities of my father, and his father, and his father's father, might be reigning in my spirit man. Also, their iniquities coupled with my own will be passed down to my children and their children's children to come.

After King David went into Bathsheba, the wife of Uriah, he prayed to the father to forgive him of his adulterous behavior. David blamed his sexually immoral behavior on the iniquities and sin that reigned in his carnal flesh. This is what David cried to God, admitting his wrongdoing with Uriah's wife: "Behold, I was brought forth in iniquity, and in sin my mother conceived me" (Ps 51: 5). David is declaring to the Lord that these two very viable curses overwhelmed his better judgment and caused him to commit this act against his servant Uriah.

Paul also makes a similar declaration regarding sin in Romans, chapter 7: "For I know that in me (that is, in my flesh) nothing good dwells; for to will is present to me, but how to perform what is good I do not find. For the good that

I will to do, I do not do; but the evil I will not to do, that I practice. Now if I do what I will not to do, it is no longer I that do it, but sin that dwells in me" (vv. 18 – 20).

Sin is a seed that roots in the flesh when we transgress the law of God, for the flesh becomes the tool that brings forth all our misdeeds. The body can be used in righteousness or in disobedience, and the penalty for this disobedience is sin, which in most cases is leading to death.

So then, Abel's spirit, being brought forth from his mother's womb, laden down with the iniquities of his father, Adam, would not be able to abide in the heavenly realm with the Father. He would have to share in the same fate as the fallen angels who defiled themselves in disobedience. Abel's spirit would have to descend into the lower parts of the earth prepared for Satan and his minions—Hades. Unlike the fallen angels who are kept prisoner under this realm of darkness in a conscious state, man's spirit falls into a perpetual sleep till the end of time (Jude 6; Dan. 12:1 – 3). He will awake to either everlasting life or to eternal contempt.

There are many references in the scripture regarding this place of rest. Jesus tells us in Matthew, chapter 12, that He Himself would descend into this place of darkness. "For as Jonah was three day and three nights in the belly of the great fish, so will the Son of Man be three days and three nights in the heart of the earth" (v. 40).

Paul also wrote of our Lord's descent into the realm of darkness in his epistle to the Ephesians: "(Now this, 'He descended'—what does it mean but that He also first descended in to the lower parts of the earth? He who descended is also the One who ascended far above all the heavens, that He might fill all things)" (4:9 – 10).

Job describes Hades as "a land as dark as darkness itself…" (Jb. 10:22). Job also wrote of the descent to the gates of Sheol (Hades) in chapter 17:6. These bars or gates of Hades are also mentioned by Jonah when describing his own personal descent into this land of no return. "Jonah was swallowed by the great fish, and remained in the...belly of the fish three days and three nights" (Jonah 1:17). He refers to his water grave as the belly of Sheol (Hades). Once swallowed by the fish, he describes how the waters surround him even to the extinction of his soul (life), as the seaweeds wrapped around his head. Then, once his flesh succumbed to the waters, his spirit began its descent in to the abyss. This is what Jonah recalls of his decent into Hades: "I went down to the bottoms and very roots of the mountains; the earth with its bars closed behind me forever. Yet You have brought up my life from the pit and corruption. O Lord my God" (Jonah 2:6).

He goes on to say that as he descended, and even when he reached this place of no return, he continued to pray and admonish God, and the Lord remembered him. "And the Lord spoke to the fish, and it vomited out Jonah upon dry land" (v. 10 Amp.). Once Jonah's flesh was spewed up from the mouth of the fish and was once again on dry land, his spirit returned to him and he was made whole.

In Luke, chapter 8, we have an example of the spirit returning to the body of a young girl who had succumbed to sickness. She was the daughter of Jairus, a ruler of the synagogue, who went to Jesus in hopes that He could rid his 12 year-old daughter of her sickness. As Jesus accompanied Jairus to his home the throng delayed Him. As Jesus was still addressing the crowd, a man came to Jairus and told him that his daughter had died, and there was no need to trouble Jesus any longer. "But when Jesus heard it, He answered him, saying, 'Do not be afraid; only believe and she will be made well" (v. 50). When Jesus entered the house, everyone was mourning for the child, but Jesus said, "...Do not weep; she is not dead, but sleeping" (v. 52).

What did Jesus mean that "she is not dead, but sleeping"? Death and sleep are synonyms with one another according to the teachings of Jesus and His apostles. Jesus made this overtly clear to His disciples in the gospel of John, as they contended with Him about returning to Bethany to awaken Lazarus (the brother of Mary and Martha) from his sleep. "These things He said, and after that He said, 'Our friend Lazarus sleeps, but I must go that I may wake him up. Then His disciples said, 'Lord, if he sleeps he will get well.' However, Jesus spoke of his death, but they thought that He was speaking about taking rest in sleep. Then Jesus said to them plainly, 'Lazarus is dead'" (Jn. 11:14)

The apostle Paul also used sleep when speaking of the deceased. "For if we believe that Jesus died and rose again, even so God will bring with Him those who sleep in Jesus. For this we say to you by the word of the Lord, that we who are alive and remain until the coming of the Lord will by no means precede those who are asleep" (1 Thes. 4:14 – 15).

Why use sleep as an analogy for the present state of the deceased? The answer is because corruption and decay of physical death is present with us all, but the spirit is not in a state of corruption or decay when it leaves the body. It is in a state of perpetual rest. Hence the phrase "Rest in Peace".

Chapter 5

The Death of Adam:

"After he begot Seth, the days of Adam were eight hundred years; and he had sons and daughters. So all the days that Adam lived were nine hundred and thirty years; and he died" (Gen. 5:4 – 5).

What does it mean that our father, Adam, lived 930 years? Are these literal years? Yes. We must remember who Adam was—the son of God—and his flesh was never to see corruption. He had eaten from the Tree of Life for nearly a millennium before being cast from the Garden. Then, 930 years later, Adam's flesh succumbed to the death. "...For out of it you were taken [the ground]; for dust you are, and to dust you shall return" (Gen. 3:19).

Verse 4 of Genesis tells us that Adam sired many sons and daughters in the 930 years from the time he was cast from the Garden to the time of his death. It would be from the lineage of Adam's third son, Seth, and Seth's descendant Noah, that all humankind would be saved and redeemed.

The Birth of Our First Savior, Noah:

"...Noah, the son of Lamech, the son of Methuselah, the son of Enoch, the son of Jared, the son of Mahalalel, the son of Cainen, the son of Enosh, the son of Seth, the son of Adam, the son of God" (Lk. 3:36 – 38).

Noah was the tenth generation from Adam. He was born to Lamech, his father, about the time of Adam's death. This meant that he was born about 930 years after the exile, or, according to man's calendar, the year 3070 BC. Noah would live 500 years before he begot his three sons Shem, Ham, and Japheth. His sons were born in an age when the earth was overrun with man's perversions and disobedience against the precepts of the Most High. Man's heart was becoming more and more perverse in the sight of the Most High.

Also in Noah's time, as the daughters of men multiplied on the earth, the Father allowed His sons, the angels, to come down to the earth and take the daughters of men as wives. And from the loins of the angels came forth men of valor, men of renown. This union brought forth men of great stature—giants. I believe the Lord allowed these unions, firstly because of free will: "...that the sons of God saw the daughters of men, that they were beautiful..." (Gen. 6:2). It was by God's own precepts (the law of marriage) that made these unions acceptable in His sight. It was better to allow these unions than to have His sons burning in desire for the daughters of men. Secondly, the sons of God were pure in spirit, lacking the iniquities of their earthly counterparts. From the loins of the angels came forth offspring of pure spirits who would go forth in the earth, marry the daughters of men, and bring forth generations of men who were free of the inherited curse of iniquity carried down by the descendants of Adam.

Unfortunately, the earth was so overrun with corruption that even these men of renown would also fall victim to what was to come upon the earth. "Then the Lord saw that the wickedness of man was great in the earth, and that every intent of the thoughts of his heart was only evil continuously. And the Lord was sorry that He had made man on the earth, and he was grieved in His heart. So the Lord said, 'I will destroy man whom I have created from the face of the earth, both man and beast, creeping things and birds of the air, for I am sorry that I have made them.' But Noah found grace in the sight of the Lord" (Gen. 5:6)

"...Noah was just man, perfect in his generation. Noah walked with God"

In the midst of this overt corruption, this one man walked in obedience to God. And because of this one man's righteous behavior before heaven and man, God spared Noah and his children from the destruction to come. The Lord commissioned Noah to build an ark of gopher wood to shelter him, his wife, and his three sons and their wives from the waters that would soon flood the entire earth and bring death to all flesh that walked, crawled, and flew over the surface of the earth. These were the Lord's specifications to build his ark: "Make yourself an ark of gopherwood; make rooms in the ark and cover it inside and outside with pitch. And this is how you should make it: The length of the ark shall be three hundred cubits [about 450 feet), and its width fifty cubits [about 75 feet], its height thirty cubits [about 45 feet]. You shall make a window for the ark, and you shall finish to a cubit [about 18 inches], from above; and set the door of the ark in its side. You shall make it with lower, second, and third decks" (vv. 14 – 16) Some believe that Noah was about 500 years old when God set him out on this very daunting task of constructing the ark. I believe his sons, at the time of the ark's construction, were well into adulthood, which would mean, according to the scriptures, that Noah may have been closer to six hundred years old (Ref. Gen. 5:32).

So then, four men took on the task of building a sea-worthy vessel about 450 feet long, 75 feet wide, and over four stories tall. That's quite an undertaking, especially for Noah, a man more than half a millennium old.

At the age of sixteen, I dropped out of school and started a career in carpentry. By the age of twenty-one, I became the lead man of a framing crew building homes. This led me to owning my own construction and Development Company. Over the course of ten years, I may have framed and/or completed close to one hundred homes, from Boston to

Martha's Vineyard. Each home may have averaged between twelve hundred to twenty five hundred square feet. And from start to finish, each home took an average of several months to complete. In every stage of construction, we used power tools such as circular saws, power drills, pneumatic nail guns, and table saws. These are just several of the most commonly used power tools you would find on today's construction sites.

Now let us go back 4520 years to the time of Noah to see what type of tools Noah would have had at hand to construct this massive vessel. We would probably find several types of hand axes with metal heads to crop down the gopherwood trees; a few crude metal blade saws to cut the lumber to length; maybe some type of metal blade instrument for debarking the trees; some crude hammers and metal fasteners (nails); ropes and pulleys for moving and lifting beams into place (probably powered by oxen or donkeys); and some crudely-made wooden slosh buckets and bushes made from the tails of donkeys to carry and spread the pitch (tar) along the lengths of lumber to seal each and every seam from water leakage.

With just a small variety of primitive tools at hand, Noah and his sons constructed a vessel that even by today's standards would be a costly and lengthy undertaking. The actual living area square footage of this three-story vessel may have exceeded fifty thousand square feel. This would mean that the living space of the ark was equivalent to thirty or more of the residential homes that I've built in the past. I would have to at least agree with some of my contemporaries, knowing how daunting of a task it was to construct this massive vessel in Noah's time, that the ark was a decades-long construction.

The Great Flood:

"Noah was six hundred years old when the floodwaters were on the earth" (Gen. 7:6).

At the age of six hundred, Noah and his sons completed the ark. The Lord instructed Noah to go into the ark and take with him: his wife, his sons, and his sons' wives; seven of each clean animal, a male with its female; two of every unclean animal, a male with its female; seven each of the birds of the air, a male with its female; and every other kind of creature that crawls upon the face of the earth. So then, two by two every creature that walked, crawled, and flew over the face of the earth followed Noah into the ark. For the Lord had said to Noah, "For after seven more days I will cause it to rain on the earth forty days and forty nights, and I will destroy from the face of the earth all living things that I had made" (7:4) And it came to pass that after seven days that the rains began to fall on the earth and the Lord shut him (Noah) in the ark, sealing the door behind him.

What is commonly taught by the church of this epic event is that the rains fell on the earth for forty days and forty nights and when the rains ceased, Noah, his family, and every creature that entered the ark with him made a quick exit. Unfortunately for Noah and his family, that wasn't the case. Noah, his family, and the all of the creatures that followed him into the ark were actually sealed up in the ark for an astounding twelve months and ten days. Verse 11 gives us the exact date that Noah entered the ark: "In the six hundredth year of Noah's life, in the second month, the seventh day of the month...the foundations of the great deep were broken up [the continental plates], and the windows of heaven were open.

If we were to numerically record this date, we would write it as 2-17-600, just as we would write a more modern date of 2-17-2013. Why were these dates of the flood recorded with such accuracy?

In the first two millennia of man, the passing of time was determined by the age of the fathers. Adam lived for 930 years from the time he was exiled from the Garden until his death. Time, in the first millennium was kept according to

Adam's age, for example: "And Adam lived one hundred and thirty years, and begot…Seth" (Gen. 5:3). You see, Adam's age of 130 years marks a date, not only in his time but also in our historical dateline. According to man's calendar, the one hundred and thirtieth year of Adam's life would be the year 3870 BC. Adam's death at 930 years old would mark the ending of the first millennium of man, which would be the year 3070BC of our modern calendar. With Adam no longer walking on the earth, time would be kept by the days of Noah. The scripture tells us that Noah was six hundred years old at the time the floodwaters were on the earth. So, this would mean that the flood occurred about fifteen hundred and thirty years after Adam's exile from the Garden, which would translate into the year 2470 BC.

Noah kept a very accurate account of events that occurred during the time he was sealed in the ark. By keeping track of the days, weeks, and months that passed from the time he entered the ark to his somewhat grand departure, Noah reveals several key dates in the biblical record that will become very prevalent in the end-time prophecies of the Book of Revelation. For example, the dates recorded in verses 4, 5, 13, and 14 of chapter 8 also align with the breaking of the first four of the seven seals of the scroll that released the four horsemen of the Apocalypse, mentioned in chapters 5 through 7 of Revelations. These four dates span a time of two hundred and twenty days.

Noah entered the ark on the seventeenth day of the second month from his six hundredth birthday (2-17-600). He, his family, and all the creatures that entered the ark with him exited the ark on the twenty-seventh day of the second month of his six hundredth and first birthday (2-27-601). This means that Noah, his family, and all the creatures who were saved from the floodwaters, were sealed up in the ark for one year and ten days (370 days according to Noah's lunar calendar) before they walked, crawled, and flew again over the dry land. And Noah built an altar and took of every clean animal and fowl and sacrificed them to God. "So God blessed Noah and his sons, and said to them, 'Be fruitful and multiply, and fill the earth'" (Gen. 9:1).

The Lord also made a covenant with Noah and his sons on the day they exited the ark, saying" "And as for Me, behold, I establish My covenant with you and with your descendants after you, and with every living creature that is with you: the birds, the cattle, and every beast of the earth with you, of all that go out of the ark, every beast of the earth...I set My rainbow in the cloud, and it shall be for the sign of the covenant between Me and the earth...and I will remember My covenant..." and "...the waters shall never again become a flood to destroy all flesh" (Gen. 9:8 – 15)

The New Beginning:

So Noah went out from the ark—him, his wife, and his sons with their wives. If was commissioned by the Lord, to Noah's sons Shem, Ham, and Japheth to multiply on the earth and replenish it. The Lord also blessed every creature who came out of the ark with Noah and his family to do the same. Multiply and bring forth offspring of every kind. And both man and beast cleaved to the spoken word of God and began to multiply on the face of the earth.

Chapter 6

The Earth Divided:

Shem, the son of Noah, begot his first son, Arphaxad, two years after exiting the ark. Shem was one hundred years old at the time of Arphaxad's birth. Shem lived another five hundred years and begot many more sons and daughters. Arphaxad lived thirty-five years and begot his first son, Salah. Arphaxad lived another four hundred three years and begot many more sons and daughters. Salah lived thirty years and begot Eber. Eber lived thirty-four years and begot Peleg. It is recorded in Genesis 10:25 that in the days of Peleg the earth was divided. But what does it mean that the earth was divided? Many theologians and scholars over the centuries have interpreted this one verse with much bias, referencing the story of Babel in chapter 11:1 – 9.

Nimrod was born to the third generation from the Flood, to Cush, the son of Ham (the son of Noah). He became a mighty person on the earth, becoming king over all its inhabitants. Under Nimrod's rule, the people went out and built many cities. One was called Babel. It was built on the plains of Shimar. One day Nimrod went out to the people and commissioned them to construct a tower whose top would reach the heavens. "But the Lord came down to see the city and the tower which the sons of men had built. And the Lord said, 'Indeed the people are one and they all have one language, and this is what they begin to do; now nothing that they propose to do will be withheld from them. Come, let us go down there and confuse their language, that they may not understand one another's speech'. So the Lord scattered them abroad from there over the face of all the earth, and they ceased building the city" (vv. 5 – 8).

Now with Peleg being born to the fourth generation after the Flood, and living to a good old age of two hundred and thirty-nine, he was one of the many children of Noah who did walk on the earth at the time of Nimrod, when the Lord and the angels came down and confused the language of the people and scattered them across the face of the earth. However, I, as many other devout Creationists, believe this particular scripture holds a dual meaning. It's written in verse 8, that the Lord "...scattered them abroad over the face of all the earth [Pangaea]..." In my interpretation, this means that the earth is still whole at this time. Yes, the people were scattered abroad to every corner of the earth, but this was an undertaking and a pilgrimage. The sons of Noah packed up their belongings, their wives, children, and livestock, and walked out of the city of Babel and the plains of Shinar. And once the descendants of Noah began to settle in these new lands of Pangaea, this once supercontinent began to separate and divide in to the seven continents of today.

Let us look back to Genesis 7:11, where it is recorded that on the day that Noah entered the ark "...the foundations of the great deep were broken up..." I interpret this scripture in this way: On that day when Noah entered the ark, the Lord literally shook the foundation of the earth (Pangaea) to its very core. This would have caused the massive continent to begin to fracture and separate into the continental plates.

I believe the same force that the Lord used to bring the super-continent up from the ocean floor on the third day of Creation was also used in this millennium to separate it. We must also take some other facts into consideration when trying to rationalize this super-continent theory and its division into the seven continents. Prior to 1492 AD, the Americas were unknown to our European ancestors, who were also under the belief that the world was flat. So, we can safely say that somewhere between the dates of 2369 and 2130 BC (the life of Peleg), when the earth was divided until the time that Columbus set sail in 1492 AD, we had no world maps to record and document the actual speed that the continents were drifting apart from one another.

Like many of my fellow creationists, I believe that the continents separated at a fairly rapid speed when first divided. I am also theorizing that by the time of Christ Jesus the continents had slowed to nearly a crawl and the division of the earth was nearly completed. I read several years ago that the east coast of North America and the western shores of Europe are still drifting apart from one another at a rate of about six inches per year. Judging by this slow rate of movement, we can see that the earth is still not willing to come to a halting rest.

The separation of the continents was God's "master plan" to create diversity on the earth. From the Incas to the Mayans to the indigenous peoples of South America to the Hopi Indians of North America to the Eskimo and all the peoples throughout Europe, Asia, Africa, and the indigenous people of the continent of Australia, they are all descendants of the sons of Noah. We walk the earth today speaking in different tongues with great variations in our skin tones and cultures. Fanatical differences in our religious beliefs and governmental structures exist. Regardless of all this very well planned diversity, we all descend from one place and from one Father, which makes us all the children of Noah.

The Birth of Abraham:

Peleg was the fourth generation from the Flood born to the sons of Shem. Abraham was the ninth generation born to the sons of Shem. He was born to his father, Terah, two hundred ninety-two years after the Flood. Abraham would be the nineteenth generation born to the sons of Adam, about 1822 years after Adam's exile from the Garden (which means Abraham would have been born in the year 2178 BC).

Abraham dwelt in the city of Ur, in the lands of the Chaldeans, with his father, Terah, and his two brothers, Nahor and Haran. While living amongst the people of Ur,

Abraham's brother, Haran, died leaving a son named Lot. The time had come for Terah to depart from the city of Ur to go to the land of Canaan. With him he took Abraham (who was called Abram) and his daughter Sarah (who was called Sari), who he gave to Abram to be his wife. As they journeyed to the land of the Canaanites, they came upon Haran and dwelt there for a time. While dwelling in Haran, Terah succumbed to his old age and died. Terah was two hundred five years old at the time of his death. Following Terah's death, the Lord came and spoke with Abram, saying: "Get out of your country, from your family and from your father's house, to the land that I will show you. I will make you a great nation; I will bless you and make your name great; and you shall be blessed. I will bless those who bless you, and curse him who curses you; and in you all the families of the earth shall be blessed" (Gen. 12:1 – 4). So, Abram, in the faith of God, departed from Haran with his wife, Sari, and all the people and possessions that he had acquired while in Haran. His nephew Lot also followed with him. Abraham was seventy-five years old when he set out from Haran to the land of the Canaanites.

At this time our father Noah had already succumbed to his old age. Noah lived three hundred fifty years after the Flood and died at the age of nine hundred fifty (about 2120 BC).

The Lord came again to Abram when he had reached the land of Canaan, saying: "To your descendants I will give this land. And there he built an alter to the Lord, who had appeared to him" (Gen. 12:7).

During the following years, Abraham, along with his nephew Lot, traversed the lands between Canaan and Egypt several times, accumulating much wealth, livestock, and followers. In fact, they both grew so great in wealth that Abraham and his nephew Lot's herdsmen were in constant strife over lands and territories. So, the time came for Abraham and Lot to separate from one another. "And Lot lifted his eyes and saw all the plain of Jordan, that was well watered everywhere (before the Lord destroyed Sodom and Gomorah) like the garden of the Lord, like the land of Egypt as you go to Zoar" (Gen. 13:10).

So, Lot took all his livestock with his herdsmen and their possession and headed for the plains of the Jordan. The Lord came to Abraham again after Lot departed from him to reassure him of his inheritance. He spoke to Abram, saying, "Lift your eyes now and look from the place where you are—northward, southward, eastward, and westward; for all the land which you see I give to you and your descendants forever" (vv. 14 – 15). Abram departed from that place and pitched his tent in Hebron. As time passed, Sari was still barren and unable to give an heir to Abram, so Sari gave to Abram her Egyptian servant and slave, Hagar, as a concubine that she may bear Abram a son and heir. "So Hagar bore Abram a son; and Abram named his son, whom Hagar bore, Ismael" (Gen. 16:15).

Abram was eighty-six years old when Hagar bore Ismael to him. He loved his son, because in Ismael Abram had an heir. However, Abram would soon come to find out that Ismael, being the first and only son to be born of his loins, was not to be heir to all his possessions and lineage. Another was to be born to him by his wife, Sari, in her old age. Ismael grow strong in the tent of his mother Hagar. Nevertheless, strife and jealousy divided the tents of Sari and Ismael's mother Hagar. It was Sari who gave her servant Hagar to her husband Abram, but once Hagar conceived in her womb, Sari's countenance turned to one who had hate and contempt in her heart. Sari became an evil taskmaster to her servant Hagar.

We see this same theme replaying over and over again in the pages of the Old Testament. Our forefathers taking on multiple wives and not being able to fulfill the needs of each individual wife, causing strife between their spouses, concubines, and even their children. We either find a wife (such as Leah, Jacob's first wife) filled with insecurities and the feeling of being unloved or one like Rachael (Jacob's second wife), who was the apple of her husband's eye and received all the love and attention of her husband. Let us not forget the children of these unstable polygamous unions.

Our father Jacob married both Leah and Rachel, the daughters of Laben, his mother's brother. Each of his wives gave him their servants as concubines and each bore him children. His sons and daughters dwelt in four separate households (tents) basically detached from one another's household. We will see in the following chapter that the children of Jacob, who were reared in separate tents, held much contempt toward one another.

I, myself, neither am an advocate for polygamy, nor am I an advocate against such unions. My father married four women in his lifetime and three of his four wives bore him children. My mother also remarried and had a son. I have two brothers who were born to my father's second wife and a sister who was born to my father's fourth wife. I also have a stepsister, who is the daughter of my father's fourth wife from a previous marriage. I am the oldest of my siblings from my father's first wife. Both my sister Maria and I share the same mother and had grown up in the same household as my brother Carl (my stepfather's son). So, my own life experience of growing up in a similar type of polygamist lifestyle helps me understand the plight and the consequences of these multiple unions.

The Son of Promise:

When Abraham was at the age of ninety-nine years old, the Lord appeared to him, saying, "I am the Almighty God; walk before me and be blameless". The Lord also said to Abraham, "No longer shall your name be called Abram, but your name shall be Abraham; for I have made you a father of many nations". Then "God said to Abraham, 'As for Sari your wife...Sarah shall be her name...I will bless her, and she shall be the mother of many nations; kings of peoples shall be from her'. Then Abraham fell on his face and laughed, and said in his heart, 'Shall a child be born to a man who is one hundred years old? And shall Sarah, who is ninety years old, bear a child?'" (Gen. 17:1, 5, 15 – 17).

After hearing the Lord's proclamation concerning Sarah's conception, Abraham petitioned the Lord on behalf of his son, Ismael, and the Lord answered him: "'No. Sarah your wife shall bear you a son, and you shall call his name Isaac; I will establish My covenant with him for an everlasting covenant and with his descendants after him'" (Gen. v. 19). And concerning Ismael, the Lord said that He would bless him and make him fruitful, and multiply him exceedingly on the earth. As for Isaac, the Lord told Abraham that Sarah would give birth to him at a set time next year.

The Covenant Established:

Then the Lord commissioned Abraham to circumcise every male of his people in the foreskin of their penis. So Abraham went out and circumcised every male of his household, both free and slave. The Lord also commissioned Abraham, as a sign of the covenant between him and his descendants, to circumcise every male child when he turns eight days of age. "He who is eight days old among you shall be circumcised, every male child in your generation, he who is born in your house or bought with money from any foreigner who is not your descendant" (v. 12)

This covenant of circumcision is still practiced today by the Jewish people, who are direct descendants of Abraham in the flesh. It is an everlasting covenant that will be fulfilled on the eighth day of man—the second resurrection of the dead, as is recorded in Daniel 12:2: "And many of those who sleep in the dust of the earth shall awake, some to everlasting life, some to shame and everlasting contempt".

The Promise Reconfirmed:

A time had come when the violence of Sodom and Gomorrah had reached into the heavens. The cities were filled with idolatries and sexual immoralities, such as homosexuality, bisexuality, lesbianism, pedophilia, bestiality, rape, and other creations of filth to satisfy the people's carnal desires. One day while Abraham was sitting at the door of his tent, he saw three men standing near him and ran after them. He fell at their feet knowing they were from God. Abraham asked them to stay and sit under the shade of a tree while he bathed their feet in water. Then he ran in to the tent to have Sarah fix the angels of the Lord some morsels of bread and meat. The Lord was among the three angels and said to Abraham, "I will certainly return to you according to the time of life, and behold, Sarah your wife shall have a son". Sarah heard what the Lord had said to Abraham and she laughed to herself, saying, "After I have grown old, shall I have pleasure, my lord being old also?" The Lord knew Sarah had laughed and said to herself "Shall I surely bear a child, since I am old?" He asked of Abraham and Sarah, "Is anything too hard for the Lord?" But Sarah, being afraid in the presence of the Lord, denied that she had laughed, and the Lord retorted, "No, but you did laugh!"

The angels rose to their feet and looked towards Sodom and the Lord said "Shall I hide from Abraham what I am doing?" Then the Lord revealed to Abraham His intentions for Sodom and Gomorrah. The Lord told Abraham that the outcry against both Sodom and Gomorrah was very great, and He and His angels had come down to pass judgment on these cities. Abraham, knowing that his nephew Lot and his people were dwelling in Sodom, began to contend with the Lord over the righteousness that may still be found in both Sodom and Gomorrah. As a result the Father agreed that if just five righteous men were found in Sodom, that he would not totally destroy the city. Abraham's argument, however, was for naught, for as soon as the two angels entered the city of Sodom, they were met by a throng of men willing to take them by force to have them in a sexual manner (believing them to be men, not angels). In an attempt to calm the madness and lust of the men of Sodom, Lot offered his two virgin daughters to the crowd, but they were refused. The men of Sodom lusted for the flesh of men, so the offering of the daughters was not a feasible exchange for the two angels in Lot's company. The practice of homosexuality was so prevalent in the loins of these men that the natural use of a woman had become unappealing to them. Men with men, lying with one another, doing what is truly abominable in the sight of God were common practice in Sodom and Gomorrah.

While Lot was still contending with the throng, the two angels struck the men of Sodom with blindness. Then the angels took Lot, his wife, and his two daughters by the hands and led them out of the city. "So it came to pass, when they had brought them outside, that they said 'Escape for your life! Do not look behind you or stay anywhere in the plain. Escape to the mountains, lest you be destroyed'" (Gen. 19:17). But Lot's wife did not heed the instructions of the angels and looked back over her shoulder upon the destruction "...and she became a pillar of salt" (v. 26)

The cities Sodom and Gomorrah were destroyed three hundred ninety-one years after the Flood (about 2079 BC).

The Birth of Isaac:

"And the Lord visited Sarah as He had said, and the Lord did for Sarah as He had spoken. For Sarah conceived and bore Abraham a son in his old age, at the set time of which God had spoken to him. And Abraham called the name of his son who was born to him—whom Sarah bore to him—Isaac. Then Abraham circumcised his son Isaac when he was eight days old, as God had commanded him.

Now Abraham was one hundred years old when his son Isaac was born to him. And Sarah said, 'God has made me laugh, and all who hear will laugh with me'. She also said, 'Who would have said to Abraham that Sarah would nurse children? For I have borne him a son in his old age'" (Gen. 21:1 – 7). Isaac was born three hundred ninety-two years after the Flood (about 2078 BC).

It was not long after Isaac's birth that Sarah turned her attention to Hagar, and Hagar's son Ismael, saying to Abraham: "Cast out this bondwoman and her son; for the son of this bondwoman shall not be heir with my son...Isaac" (v. 10). Sarah's demand displeased Abraham because he loved his son Ismael. Nonetheless, Abraham took heed to her words and cast Hagar and Ismael from the face of Sarah. However, as the Lord promised Abraham, He made Ismael a great nation.

Sarah's death:

Sarah was one hundred twenty-seven years old at the time of her death. She died in Hebron, in the land of Canaan. After her death, Abraham purchased a cave from the sons of Heth for four hundred shekels of silver and buried Sarah in the cave. This would also become the tomb of Abraham and his children.

At the time of Sarah's death, Abraham was about the age of one hundred thirty-seven, meaning Isaac was nearing forty years of age. It was time to send his servant to the house of Nahor (his brother), in Mesopotamia (Abraham's homeland), to find a suitable bride for Isaac among his relatives. When his servant same upon the land of Nahor, he met Rebekah, the granddaughter of Nahor, by a well of water. Once the servant introduced himself to be Abraham's trusted servant, Rebekah brought him to her father Bethuel and brother Laban. After hearing the words of Abraham's servant, Laban and Bethuel sent Rebekah with Abraham's servant to the land of Canaan to marry Isaac.

Isaac took Rebekah for his wife, but Rebekah had trouble conceiving. For years, Isaac pleaded with the Lord regarding his wife's fertility problem and, after nearly twenty years of wedlock, Rebekah conceived twins in her womb. "But the children struggled together within her; and she said, 'If all is well, why am I like this?' So she went to inquire of the Lord.

And the Lord said to her,

'Two nations are in your womb, two peoples shall be separated, from your body; one people shall be stronger than the other, and the older shall serve the younger'" (Gen. 25: 22 – 23).

Isaac was sixty years old when Rebekah gave birth to Esau and Jacob. Jacob was born to the last generation of the second day of man (the ninth millennium). He was born 452 years after the Flood of Noah, about the year 2018 BC.

The Death of Abraham:

Fifteen years after the birth of the sons of Isaac, Jacob and Esau, Abraham succumbed to his old age and died at the age of one hundred seventy-five years old. This would have been about the year 2003 BC, right on the cusp of a new millennium. Both Isaac and Ismael buried their father Abraham in the cave of Machpelah, alongside his wife Sarah.

We end this second millennium of man with the birth of Jacob (who would also be called Israel), and the death of our most beloved father, Abraham. Abraham is respectfully referred to as the father of faith. He was a man whom was loved by God and revered by all his contemporaries. Abraham walked in perfect faith in the sight of God, and his obedience and perseverance has been a reward to all who have decided to walk in his same footsteps. Amen.

From the time Adam was cast from the Garden of Eden until the birth of Jacob, Abraham's grandson, who was born to the twenty-first generation from Adam, is a two thousand year period. I refer to it as "The Reign of the Fathers". Many of my contemporaries separate and divide these timelines and events into dispensational periods. Despensationalism was derived by scholars and theologians in the eighteenth century to try and bring some divine order to the recorded timelines of biblical records. However, I believe that dispensationalism has left us Christians scratching our heads. On the other hand, I believe that categorizing these biblical timelines and events under the reigning times of our forefathers is much more practical and beneficial to my students. For example, let us begin to review the first week of Creation.

The first six days of creation recorded in Genesis chapter one covers the first six thousand years of the Lord's Calendar of Creation. The last and seventh day of the first week of Creation is called the Sabbath. On this day the Lord rested (Gen. 2: 1 – 3). On the eighth day of Creation, which is the first day of the second week, Adam was cast from the Garden. For 930 years, time was kept by Adam's age. From the time he was cast from the Garden until his death at the age of 930 years old. So, for 930 years of the first day of man, time was recorded in accordance with Adam's age. Then for another 950 years, time was recorded in accordance with Noah's age until his death 350 years after the Flood.

However, at the time of Noah's death, man's lifespan began to decrease at a very rapid rate. Abraham died at the good old age of one hundred seventy-five. Isaac lived to the age of one hundred eighty years. And Jacob was one hundred forty-seven years old at the time of his death. By the time of Moses, about the fifteenth century BC, man's life expectancy was about seventy years. This is mentioned in the Prayer of Moses, recorded in Psalm 90:10. "The days of our lives are seventy years; and if by reason of strength they are eighty years..."

Why such a drastic decrease in man's lifespan? In the time of Noah, before the Flood, the Lord decreed that man, because he is flesh, shall not strive with Him forever: "yet his days shall be one hundred and twenty years" (Gen. 6:3). Thus, from the time of Noah's death (the year 2120 BC), time was kept by the passing of generations—not the generations born to men, but by the passing generations of time. Each generation of time regarding the biblical record spans a forty-year period. We see a reference to this forty year generation in Psalm 95:10 – 11: "For forty years I was grieved with that generation, and said, 'It is a people who go astray in their hearts, and they do not know My ways'. So I swore in My wrath, 'They shall not enter My rest'." Here the Lord is speaking of his children Israel, who He just had taken out of bondage in Egypt. Because of disbelief and disobedience, the Lord had that generation, who walked out of Egypt; wander in the wilderness for forty years until that entire generation, except Joshua and Caleb, had passed away.

Below is a review of the timeline of these first nine days (or millenniums) of Creation.

> The first week of Creation lasted: 7,000 years
> Adam lived for: 930 years (the year 3070 BC)
> Noah lived for: 950 years (the year 2120 BC)
> Abraham's generation: 40 years
> Isaac's generation: 40 years
> Jacob's generation: 40 years
> Totaling: 9,000 years (the year 2000 BC)

These are the generations born to Adam in the first two days of man. Another fifty generations of time must pass before the birth of Christ Jesus. We will cover the events of these fifty generations in chapter 7.

Chapter 7

The Reign of the 12 Patriarchs:

The scripture has revealed to us that Jacob, the son of Isaac (who is the son of Abraham), being born about the year 2018 BC, was still a very young man at the turn of the new millennium (2000 BC). He would be the last to be born to "The Reign of the Fathers" in the second millennium of man. Jacob would go on to become the founding patriarch of the twelve tribes of Israel. In the time of Moses, when he went to the top of Mount Horeb (the mountain of God), the Lord identified Himself to Moses from the burning bush in his manner: "I am the God of your father—the God of Abraham, the God of Isaac, and the God of Jacob..." (Ex. 3:6). It would be Jacob, the second son of Isaac, who would be the heir to carry down the blessings of Abraham through his loins, ensuring that all the nations of the earth will be blessed by and through Israel.

In Hebrew, Jacob's name is said to have been taken for the simile of the word *usurper*, which is defined as one who seizes and holds (a position, office, power, etc.) by force or without legal right. We will see why such a name was attributed to this great patriarch in these following scriptures.

Esau, being the eldest son of Isaac, was to inherit and possess all of Isaac's wealth, including the right of lineage, at his death. Jacob, however, being able to outwit his unruly older brother, bought Esau's birthright for a piece of bread and a bowl of lentil soup (Gen. 25:29 – 32). To add even more insult to his brother Esau's already injured and unredeemable birthright, Jacob also went and stole his blessing from the hands of his father Isaac.

Isaac, being of an old age, weak, and almost blind, called Esau to him to lay hands upon Esau to give him the blessing of the first-born son, which rightfully belonged to him. Rebekah, Isaac's wife, overheard the words that Isaac spoke to her son Esau and went and told Jacob. Isaac commissioned Esau to go out and catch and cook him fresh game as he, Isaac, loved to eat. Isaac instructed Esau to bring it to him before he blessed him. While Esau was out hunting for Isaac's food, Jacob slipped into Isaac's tent wearing his brother's clothes, disguising himself as his brother. Isaac, after a little convincing from Jacob, Isaac believed that he was giving his blessing over to Esau. When Esau came back to Isaac's tent with the freshly cooked game that he had prepared for his father, Isaac realized what his son Jacob had done. Esau was infuriated with what Jacob had done to him and from that time Esau was determined to take his brother's life (Gen. 27:1 – 41).

With Esau's rage now against his brother Jacob and Esau being a mighty hunter and man of the field, Rebekah feared for Jacob's safety. Jacob spent his time among the tents with the elders, the women, and the children. Jacob may have been weaker in appearance than his older brother. Both Isaac and Rebekah knew that, in this particular circumstance, Jacob's wit was no match for Esau's brawn. So, Isaac blessed Jacob and sent him off to Padan Aram, to take a bride for himself from the daughters of Laban, Rebekah's brother.

Jacob's Blessing:

As Jacob traveled to Haran, the land of his grandfather Bethuel, he came to rest the night in a certain place, taking a stone and placing his head upon it to sleep. As he slept, a dream vision came to him, and in the dream the Lord came and spoke with him. "...and behold a ladder was set up on the earth, and its top reached to heaven; and there the angels of God were ascending and descending on it. And behold, the

Lord stood above it and said: 'I am the Lord God of Abraham your father and the God of Isaac; the land on which you lie I will give to you and your descendants.'" Also your descendants shall be as the dust of the earth; you shall spread abroad to the west and the east, to the north and the south; and in you and in your seed all the families of the earth shall be blessed. "Behold, I am with you and will keep you wherever you go, and will bring you back to this land; for I will not leave you until I have done what I have spoken to you'" (Gen. 28:12 – 15).

Once Jacob arose from his sleep, that very morning he took the stone that he had placed under head to sleep and anointed it with oil, consecrating it to the Lord. The place in which he had slept he called Bethel, for he knew that God was in this place. Bethel is just north of Jerusalem.

Jacob Meets Rachel:

Once Jacob arrived in the land of his grandfather, Bethuel, he came upon a well where the shepherds had been watering their sheep. As he questioned them of his uncle Laban, Rachel, Laban's daughter, was approaching the well with her father's flock. Upon seeing her, Jacob was smitten and rolled the stone from the mouth of the well so Rachel could water her father's flock. Then he approached her, introducing himself as the son of Rebekah, her father's sister. Then, kissing her cheek, he wept. Rachel was very beautiful in appearance.

When Laban met with Jacob, he asked him to stay with him and Jacob happily agreed, because his heart was now set on Rachel. "Now Jacob loved Rachel; so he said, 'I will serve you seven years for Rachel your daughter'. So Jacob served seven years for Rachel, and they seemed only a few days to him because of the love he had for her" (Gen. 29:18, 20).

When Jacob finished his seventh year he went to Laban to take Rachel as his wife, and, as promised, Laban prepared a feast for the wedding. In Hebrew tradition, the wedding festivities went on for seven days. At the end of the seven days, Rachel was to go to Jacob's tent to consummate their union. However, Laban put a veil over the face of his oldest daughter, Leah, and sent her into Jacob's tent. Jacob was deceived into taking Leah for a wife instead of Rachel, whom he had been promised. Jacob, believing that he was lying with Rachel, went into Leah, making her his wife. It was not until the morning that Jacob realized what Laban had done to him. He immediately went to Laban, saying, "What is this you have done to me? Was it not for Rachel that I have served you? Why then have you deceived me?" Then Laban explained to Jacob that in his country, it was not a practice to give the younger daughter in marriage before the older one was wed. He said to Jacob: "Fulfill her week [7 days], and we will give you this one [Rachel] also for the service which you will serve me still another seven years. So, when Leah's week of marriage was completed, Jacob also took Rachel for his wife and would have to serve his father-in-law Laban another seven years.

Jacob would serve Laban a total of twenty years in the land of Padan Aram. During that time in Haran, both his wives (Leah and Rachel) and their servants, Zilpah (Leah's servant) and Bilhah (Rachel's), bore him eleven sons and also daughters.

To Leah were born sons Reuben (the eldest), Simeon, Levi, Judah, Issachar, and Zebulun.

To Silpah were born sons Gad and Asher.

To Rachel, Joseph and also Bilpah bore two sons Dan and Naphtali.

A time came when Jacob decided to flee from the presence of his father-in-law Laban and go back to his father Isaac's house in Canaan. So Jacob set out three days ahead of Laban, fleeing from Haran with all his households, possessions, and servants and their possessions. Once Laban heard the news that Jacob had taken all his possessions, including his daughters and their children, he pursued Jacob for seven days before he finally overtook him in the mountains of Gilead (which are west of the Jordan River). Jacob was angry with Laban for pursuing him and contended with him over his household and possessions. Laban told Jacob, "...These daughters are my daughters, and these children are my children, and this flock is my flock; all that you see is mine, But what can I do this day to these my daughters or to the children whom they have borne?" (Gen. 31:43).

That day, Laban and Jacob made a covenant with one another on that mountain in Gilead. Jacob swore to Laban that he would not take any other wife to him besides his daughters. After that day, Laban returned to his land in peace, and Jacob to Esau.

Jacob Wrestles with God:

Jacob had one more obstacle remaining before he reached his father Isaac. That was his brother, Esau. Jacob had learned by his servants who went before him that Esau was coming to meet him with four hundred of his men. "So Jacob was greatly afraid and distressed; and he divided the people that were with him, and the flocks and herds and camels into two companies" (Gen.32:7). Jacob believed that his brother Esau was coming out to him in violence, so his strategy was to send the first company before him and his household, bearing gifts to Esau. If Esau did not accept his offering and attacked his first company, Jacob would have time to flee with his wives, concubines, and their children.

With a good lengthy distance between Jacob and his first company, he took his wives, concubines, and children and crossed over the ford of Jabbok, to the eastern side of the Jordan River. There, when Jacob was alone, he wrestled with a Man who he believed to be the Angel of God. Jacob wrestled the Man until the dawning of the sun and when the Man realized that he could not prevail against Jacob, the Angel touched the socket of Jacob's hip and it became out of joint. The Angel spoke to Jacob, saying, "Let me go, for the day breaks". Jacob replied, "I will not let You go unless You bless me!" So He said to him, "What is your name?" Jacob replied, "Jacob". And He said, "Your name shall no longer be called Jacob, but Israel; for you have struggled with God and with men, and have prevailed" (Gen. 32:26 -28). The Angel gave Jacob the blessing he desired and from then on Jacob walked with a limp.

Jacob Meets Esau:

When Jacob lifted up and saw Esau coming towards him with his four hundred men, Jacob prostrated himself seven times before Esau. However, Esau, when seeing his brother, ran to him and embraced him and kissed him. Esau refused his brother's presents and offerings, being a man of his own wealth.

When Jacob and his company arrived in Succoth, Jacob built himself a house. He and his people traveled through the lands of Canaan, settling about its cities. One time, when Jacob was traveling to Bethlehem, Rachel went into labor with Jacob's twelfth son, Benjamin, Joseph's brother. Rachel died giving birth and was buried in a grave that Jacob adorned with a stone pillar.

Among his travels, when Jacob reached the house of his father, in Hebron, Isaac was well advanced in age. Shortly after Jacob's arrival, Isaac succumbed to old age, being one hundred eighty years old. So, Esau and Jacob gathered all their people together and buried their father.

Joseph—The Unlikely Savior:

Joseph was born the eleventh son of Jacob and Jacob loved Joseph more than all his other sons. Jacob had a tunic made for Joseph of many colors and his other brothers (the ten before him) hated him because he was favored by their father. Joseph was also a very gifted dreamer (he received dream visions) and was also an interpreter of dreams. In fact, his brothers referred to him sarcastically as "The Dreamer".

"Now Joseph had a dream, and he told it to his brothers; and they hated him even more. So he said to them, 'Please hear this dream which I have dreamt: There we were binding sheaves in the field, then behold, my sheaf arose and also stood upright; and indeed your sheaves stood all around and bowed down to my sheaf'. And his brothers said to him, 'Shall you indeed reign over us? Or shall you indeed have dominion over us?' So they hated him even more for his dreams and for his words. Then he dreamed still another dream and told it to his brothers, and said, 'Look, I have dreamed another dream. And this time, the sun, the moon, and the eleven stars bowed down to me'. So he told it to his father and his brothers; and his father rebuked him and said to him, 'What is this dream that you have dreamed? Shall your mother and I and your brothers indeed come to bow down to the earth before you?' And his brothers envied him, but the father kept the matter in mind" (Gen. 37:5 – 11).

The heart of Joseph's brothers was set against him, being filled with hatred, jealousy and strife towards him. I believe from that point forward his older brothers plotted his demise.

One time, Joseph's brothers were tending to their father's flock in Shechem. Jacob called upon Joseph to check up on his brothers and his flocks, not as a spy but to bring back word of their well-being. So, Joseph headed to Shechem to meet his brothers where they tended their father's flocks. When Joseph's brothers spotted him coming towards them while they were in Dothan (which is further past Shechem), they plotted to kill him. Reuben, the oldest of the brothers, stopped them, and, instead, they stripped Joseph of his tunic and cast him into a pit. As Joseph's brothers sat to eat, they observed, in the distance, a caravan of Ishmaelites heading down to Egypt to sell their goods. "So Judah said to his brothers, 'What profit is there if we kill our brother and conceal his blood? Come and let us sell him to the Ishmaelites, and let not our hand be upon him, for he is our brother and our flesh.' And his brothers listened" (Gen. 37:26 – 27).

So, Judah and his brothers, for twenty shekels of silver, sold their brother Joseph into slavery. Once Joseph was in the hands of the Ishmaelites, his brothers tore his tunic and sprinkled lamb's blood upon it, making it look as it Joseph had been attacked by a wild beast. Then they took the bloodstained tunic to Jacob, their father. Recognizing the robe to be Joseph's and perceiving him dead, Jacob wept bitterly for his dead son. For Joseph was his favorite, being the first son of his love, Rachel, when Rachel was ninety years old, Jacob would lovingly refer to Joseph as "the son of his old age".

Joseph's time in Egypt:

Once the Ishmaelite's arrived in Egypt, they sold Joseph to a man named Potiphar, an Egyptian and captain of Pharaoh's guard. "The Lord was with Joseph, and he was a successful man; and he was in the house of his master the Egyptian. And his master saw that the Lord was with him and that the Lord made all he did to prosper in his hand" (Gen. 39:2 – 3). Potiphar, realizing the Lord was with Joseph, made Joseph overseer of his house and all his possessions. Joseph was highly favored by Potiphar and the Lord blessed him because of Joseph. Potiphar's wealth increased seven-fold and he became very prosperous with his house being under the authority and stewardship of Joseph.

It's recorded in the Bible that Joseph was a handsome man in both form and appearance. His good looks, however, were about to become a stumbling block for him in Potiphar's house. Potiphar's wife began to grow wanton for Joseph and she tried to proposition him by saying to him, "Lie with me". But Joseph refused her for the sake of his master Potiphar and his unwillingness to sin against God. However, her advances towards Joseph became more often until finally she tried to take him one day by constraint: "But it happened about this time, when Joseph went into the house to do work, and none of the men of the house were inside, that she caught him by his garment, saying, 'Lie with me' but he left his garment in her hand and fled outside, than she called to the men of her house and spoke to them, saying, 'See, he has brought into this house a Hebrew to mock us. He came in to me to lie with me, and I cried out with a loud voice'" (vv. 12 – 14).

Potiphar's wife, having Joseph's garment in her hands, falsely accused Joseph in the presence of her menservants and husband. Being angered with Joseph, believing his wife's false accusations, Potiphar placed Joseph where they kept the Pharaoh's prisoners. Joseph was now locked in Pharaoh's prison because of false allegations. Nonetheless, the favor of the Lord was upon Joseph in the prison. The captain of the guard favored him and gave him authority over the other prisoners and all the affairs regarding the prison. Thus, even at the lowest point of this man's life, Joseph was still made to prosper.

After some time, Pharaoh locked both his butler and chief baker in prison, who had both offended Pharaoh in some manner. The captain of the guard placed both men under the custody of Joseph. It came to pass that both the butler and the baker had dreamt one night and wanted someone to interpret their dreams. However, no one could be found.

"...So Joseph said to them, 'Do not interpretations belong to God? Tell them to me please'" (Gen. 40:8).

The butler told his dream to Joseph, and Joseph immediately interpreted it, saying: "'Now within three days Pharaoh will lift up your head and restore you to your place, and you will put pharaoh's cup in his hand according to the former manner, when you were his butler'. But remember me when it is well with you, and please show kindness to me; make mention of me to Pharaoh, and get me out of this house" (vv. 13 – 14).

Next, the chief baker told his dream to Joseph, but Joseph's interpretation of the baker's dream was not in the baker's favor. "Within three days Pharaoh will lift off your head from you and hang you on a tree; and the birds will eat your flesh from you" (v. 19). Needless to say, the baker was unpleased with Joseph's interpretation. Nevertheless, the three days passed and it was Pharaoh's birthday. During the birthday feast, he had both the butler and baker taken out of the prison and brought before him. To the butler he restored his position as cupbearer, but Pharaoh had the baker hung just as Joseph said.

Joseph becomes Governor of Egypt:

Two years had passed since the chief butler had been restored to the position of cupbearer to Pharaoh. At that time, he remembered Joseph. For Pharaoh had had a dream that was very disturbing to him. Pharaoh had sent for all the diviners of Egypt, but none were able to interpret his dream. It was at that time that the chief butler remembered Joseph, who was still in the pharaoh's prison. The butler remembered how Joseph had interpreted both his and the baker's dreams and what came to pass soon after. Pharaoh sent for Joseph that very day and told him his dream. Joseph's interpretation of his dream (dealing with the seven years of famine and plenty) and his wise council of what should be done during these years were pleasing and appealing to Pharaoh (see Genesis chapter 41 for Pharaoh's dream and its interpretations). So, Pharaoh said to his servants, speaking of Joseph, "...Can we find such a man as this, a man in whom is the Spirit of God" (Gen. 41:38).

Pharaoh, as did Potiphar and the keeper of the prison, set Joseph over his house, and made him second in charge of all the land and affairs of Egypt. Joseph was thirty years old when Pharaoh made him governor over Egypt. This would have been about the year 1898 BC. There were indeed seven years of abundance in Egypt, and Joseph took one-fifth of all the grains and produce that was grown in those seven years and stored them. Joseph was preparing Egypt for the famine that was about to come upon it and its neighboring nations. With the storage houses of Egypt full to capacity with grains, because of the warning the Lord had sent Pharaoh in his dream, Egypt would now have the capability to feed not only its own people, but any who came to Egypt in search of food. For the famine was widespread from Africa to Asia Minor.

Jacob Goes to Egypt:

It is recorded in Genesis 42 through 45 that the famine was severe in the land of Canaan, and Jacob sent his sons to Egypt to buy grain for bread. Arriving in Egypt, Joseph's brothers unwittingly came before Joseph to buy Egyptian grain. Joseph recognized his brothers, but they did not recognize him. "Joseph saw his brothers and recognized them, but he acted as a stranger to them and spoke roughly to them. Then he said to them, 'Where do you come from?' And they said, 'From the land of Canaan to buy food'...Then Joseph remembered the dreams which he dreamed about them and said to them 'You are spies! You have come to see the nakedness of the land!'" (42: 7 – 9).

This accusation of them being spies caused fear to overcome his brothers. Joseph's brothers knew that if their master's accusation was not refuted it could be a death sentence to them all. Joseph then began to test them, and his brothers began to reveal themselves to Joseph. Although Joseph spoke and treated his estranged brothers of twenty years in a rough manner, he wished them no harm.

One of Joseph's commands to his unwitting brothers was to send one of them back to Canaan to collect their younger brother Benjamin and bring him to Egypt. Prior to his command, Joseph placed his brothers in prison for three days. In order to ensure that they would return to Egypt with Benjamin, Joseph released all of them except Simeon. So, when the brothers returned to Canaan, they spoke to Jacob, their father, and told him all that had occurred in Egypt. Once Jacob heard of the Egyptian's command, he was cut to his heart, saying to his sons: "You have bereaved me: Joseph is no more, Simeon is no more, and you want to take Benjamin. All these things are against me" (42:36).

Reuben tried to convince their father to let him take Benjamin to Egypt to the Egyptian lord, but Jacob answered Reuben in this manner: "My son shall not go down with you, for his brother (Joseph) is dead, and he is left alone. If any calamity should befall him along the way in which you go, then you will bring down my gray hair with sorrow to the grave" (v. 38).

It wasn't long before the grain was all eaten and the trip back to Egypt could not be avoided. So, Jacob placed Benjamin in the hands of his brother Judah and sent him to Egypt, along with gifts for the Egyptian lord of Pharaoh. Once Judah and his brothers arrived in Egypt, they traveled right to the house of Joseph. Joseph's servants greeted his brothers and brought them into his home, washing their feet and feeding their donkeys. When Joseph arrived home he asked his brothers of their father, if he was well and living. His brothers presented him with the gifts from their father, Jacob, and then he spotted his brother Benjamin amongst the others. "Then he lifted his eyes and saw his brother Benjamin, his mother's son, and said, 'Is this your younger brother of whom you spoke to me?' And he said, 'God be gracious to you, my son'" (43:29).

Even with his brother Benjamin in his presence, Joseph still was not ready to reveal himself to his brothers. He would allow a little more calamity to fall upon them before revealing himself. Joseph went as far as seizing his brother Benjamin before revealing himself. The time came, however, and Joseph could not hold back any longer. "Then Joseph said to his brothers, 'I am Joseph; does my father still live?'...'I am Joseph your brother, whom you sold into Egypt'" (46: 3 – 4). He then revealed to his brothers the reason for their selling him into bondage, and why he was sold into slavery to Egypt: "...for God sent me before you to preserve life" (v. 5).

The famine had been in the land for nearly two years, and there were still five of the prophesied years remaining before relief would be upon the land, so Joseph commissioned his brothers to go back to the land of Canaan and collect their father, their families, and their possessions and come dwell with him in Egypt, so he could provide for Jacob, his brothers, and their families during this time of famine. Joseph's brothers departed from him and traveled back to the land of Canaan (about an eleven day journey) to collect their father and families. When Jacob heard the news of Joseph being alive and governor over all of Egypt, Jacob did not believe them. But as they told their father of all Joseph had told them, he believed and said, "...It is enough. Joseph my son is still alive. I will go and see him before I die" (45:28).

Jacob Goes to Egypt:

Jacob gathered up all his household and his sons and their households and traveled to Egypt as his son Joseph requested. "All the persons who went with Jacob to Egypt, who came from his body...were sixty-six persons in all" (v.

26). Including Joseph's household, there were seventy in all (v. 27).

When he arrived at Beersheba on his way to Egypt, Jacob made a sacrifice to the Lord. That night, as Jacob rested, the Lord spoke to him in a dream, saying, "Jacob, Jacob!" Jacob replied, "Here I am". The Lord said, "I am God, the God of your father; do not fear to go down to Egypt, for I will make you a great nation there. I will go down with you to Egypt, and I will also surely bring you up again; and Joseph will put his hands on your eyes" (Gen. 47:2 – 4).

God was with Jacob and would be with his generations until the time they were taken back up from Egypt with His own mighty hand. Why did God bring reassurance to Jacob in this dream? Upon blessing Abram, and his descendants with him, the Lord revealed to him that his descendants would go through a period of affliction for four hundred years. "Then He said, 'Know certainly that your descendants will be strangers in a land that is not theirs, and will serve them, and they will afflict them four hundred years. And also the nation whom they serve I will judge; afterwards they shall come out with great possessions'" (Gen. 15:13 – 14).

From the time Jacob went into Egypt at the age of one hundred thirty (which would have been about the year 1888 BC); his children would prosper in the land for nearly thirty years. After this thirty-year period of abundance, the Egyptians would bring Jacob's children into servitude. The Israelites would come to serve their Egyptian captors in their homes and fields, and would also become the Egyptian's main labor force behind the construction of their mighty cities and temples. Sometime between the year of his father's death and the year 1858 BC, Joseph's power in Egypt began to decline. Why? The Pharaoh—who brought Joseph from the prison and made him governor of Egypt—was probably either well-advanced in age or dead by the year 1858 BC. Whoever reigned as pharaoh in his place had no further need for Joseph and his governing skills.

Pharaoh gave to Jacob and his children the land of Goshen. Jacob dwelt in the land of Goshen for seventeen years and then he succumbed to his old age. Jacob died at the age of one hundred forty-seven years old (about the year 1871 BC). At the time of Jacob's death, Joseph would have been about fifty-seven years of age. Before Jacob took his last breath, he laid hands on both the sons of Joseph—Ephriam and Manasseh—giving them his blessing. He then laid hands on his twelve sons, blessing them as well (see Gen. Chapters 48 – 49). After blessing his children, Jacob charged them that upon his death they were to take his body back to the land of Canaan and bury him with his fathers. So, when Jacob died, his sons carried his body to Canaan and he was buried in the cave with his fathers.

After this, Joseph and his brothers returned to Pharaoh in Egypt. Joseph died years later at the age of one hundred ten. Unlike his father, however, Joseph's body was not allowed to be brought to Canaan to be buried in the cave of his fathers. Before his death, Joseph commissioned his people of Israel to bring his bones from Egypt at the time of God's visitation upon them (Gen. 50:22 – 26).

Joseph's death at the age of one hundred ten means that he lived to see the beginning of his people's four hundred years of oppression at the hands of their Egyptian taskmasters. Joseph died in roughly the year 1818 BC, and, by the dates recorded in the biblical record, I believe the children of Israel entered the four hundred years of servitude in roughly the year 1850 BC. It would not be for another three hundred twenty years that another savior would be born to the people of Israel.

We must be reminded that God is never slack in His promises. Paul wrote this of our Lord God in his epistle to the Romans: "He, that is, God, who gives life to the dead and calls those things which do not exist as though they did" (4: 17). What does this mean to those who seek Him and hold the words of His testimony in their hearts? I interpret this to mean that all that is spoken, by God, either in this time or the time to come, will come into existence in its allotted time. The Israelites, while in bondage some four hundred years, never gave up hope in the promise God had made to Abraham, their father. AMEN!

Chapter 8

The Birth of Moses:

In the three hundred twentieth year (about 1530 BC) of the Israelites' captivity in the land of Egypt, a child was born to Amram and Jochebed of the tribe of Levi. When Jochebed saw that her child was beautiful and extravagant, she hid him three months from her Egyptian captors. Why would she have to hide her newborn son? In the days of her child's birth, a pharaoh rose up in Egypt who feared that the Hebrew slaves were growing too great in numbers. It may have been that in the year 1530 BC, when Moses was born, that the Hebrews numbered close to that of their Egyptian keepers and Pharaoh feared an uprising. So, Pharaoh summoned the Hebrew midwives to him and said this to them: "When you do your duties of a midwife for the Hebrew women, and see them on the birth stools, if it is a son, then you shall kill him; but if it is a daughter, then she shall live" (Ex. 1:16).

Needless to say, Pharaoh's command to the Hebrew midwives was not implemented by these daughters of Abraham. For they feared God more than Pharaoh, their keeper. Once Pharaoh realized the midwives were unsuccessful in fulfilling his command, he ordered Egyptian people to kill the newborn sons of Israel who were born into their households. "So Pharaoh commanded all his people, saying, 'Every son who is born you shall cast into the river and every daughter you shall save alive'" (v. 22).

When the child was three months old, Jochebed constructed an ark of bulrushes (reeds) and sealed it with asphalt and pitch. She placed the child in it, and placed the ark among the reeds of the Nile River. Miriam, Moses' older sister, stayed by the river to watch what would become of her brother. It just so happened that on the day that the child was placed in the Nile, Pharaoh's daughter came down to the river to bathe. While she bathed in the river, she saw the ark and summoned her maid to retrieve the ark from the river. "And when she opened it, she saw the child, and behold, the baby wept. So she had compassion on him, and said 'This is one of the Hebrews' children'" (Ex. 2:6).

Miriam quickly approached Pharaoh's daughter and said, "Shall I go and call a nurse for you from the Hebrew women, that she may nurse the child for you?" Pharaoh's daughter said to Miriam, "Go". So Miriam ran right back to Jochebed her mother and brought her to the princess. Pharaoh's daughter unwittingly placed the child back into his mother's arms to nurse him. Jochebed not only got to mother her infant child, but also received from Pharaoh's daughter wages for her nursing. Once the child was weaned, at about the age of two or three, he was brought to Pharaoh's daughter. She became as a mother to him, naming him Moses, saying, "Because I drew him out of the waters" (v. 10).

Moses grew up in the house of Pharaoh's daughter and was educated in all the knowledge of the Egyptians. This allowed him to become a well-educated man in Egyptian mathematics and writings (hieroglyphics and Egyptian texts) and may have even mastered Hebrew writings and texts.

It is recorded that at the age of forty years old, Moses came out to his people and saw an Egyptian beating one of his Hebrew brethren. Seeing no one, that is, a witness, Moses killed the Egyptian and buried him in the sand. However, burying the Egyptian was not enough to cover up Moses' crime. The second time Moses came out to his people, he saw two of his brethren fighting. He said to the one who seemed to be in the wrong, "Why are you striking your companion?" Then the man said, "Who made you a prince and judge over us? Do you intend to kill me as you killed the Egyptian?" So

Moses was afraid and said, "Surely this is known!" (vv. 13 – 14).

Moses, fearing Pharaoh's judgment (a death sentence) upon him, fled from Egypt to the land of Midian. There he met Zipporah, the daughter of Jethro (the priest of Midian). Moses married Zipporah and she bore him two sons, Gershom and Eliezer. Moses was forty years in the desert tending the flocks of his father-in-law Jethro. One day, as he was tending Jethro's flock in Herob, by the mountain of God, Moses' heart was moved and he went up to the mountain top. There he came across a bush that was aflame with fire but was not being consumed. "And the Angel of the Lord appeared to him in a flame of fire from the midst of the bush...God called to him from the midst of the bush and said, 'Moses, Moses!' And he said 'Here I am'. Then He said, 'Do not draw near this place. Take your sandals off your feet, for the place where you stand is holy ground'. Moreover He said, 'I am the God of your father—the God of Abraham, the God of Isaac, and the God of Jacob'. And Moses hid his face, for he was afraid to look upon God" (Ex. 3:2 – 6).

The Lord told Moses that He has seen the oppression of His people at the hands of the Egyptian taskmasters and that He would send him into Egypt to deliver His people by His mighty hand. Moses asked, God, what shall I say to the children if they should ask who sent me or, "what is His name?" God said to Moses, "I Am Who I Am". He said, "Thus, you shall say to the children of Israel, 'I Am has sent me'" (vv. 13 – 14)

The Lord spoke many things to Moses on the mountain that day, and, as the Lord spoke, Moses said: "...O my Lord, I am not eloquent, neither before nor since You have spoken to your servant; but I am slow of speech and slow of tongue". The Lord replied, "'Who has made man's mouth? Or who makes the mute, the deaf, the seeing, or the blind? Have not I, the Lord?' 'Now therefore, go, and I will be with your mouth and teach you what you shall say'" (Ex. 4:10 – 12). The

Lord also appointed Aaron, Moses' brother as a spokesman for Moses.

Moses returns to Egypt:

As Moses traveled to Egypt with his wife Zipporah and his two sons, the Lord went to Aaron and told him to go out into the wilderness to meet his brother Moses. Moses and Aaron greeted each other with a kiss and then headed back for Egypt, to the house of Pharaoh.

Many historians believe that Ramses II was Pharaoh of Egypt when Moses led the Israelites out of their captivity. However, it is historical record that Ramses II reigned between the years of 1279 – 1213 BC. This date does not correspond with the biblical record. According to the Bible, The Exodus occurred about the date of 1450 BC, in the eightieth year of Moses' life. If man's historical record is correct concerning the reigns of the Egyptian pharaohs of antiquity, it would have had to have been the pharaoh Thutmus III (recorded as ruling from 1479 – 1426 BC) who was ruler of Egypt at the time of the Exodus.

So Moses and Aaron went to the pharaoh as the Lord had instructed them and said, "Thus says the Lord the God of Israel: 'Let My people go, that they may hold a feast to Me in the wilderness.'" And Pharaoh said, "Who is the Lord that I should obey His voice to let Israel go? I do not know the Lord, nor will I let Israel go'".

Pharaoh spoke roughly to Moses and Aaron when they were in his presence and Pharaoh's heart began to harden that day against the Hebrew people. On that same day, he commanded to his taskmasters that they should no longer give straw to the Hebrews to make their bricks. The straw was what bound the baked clay bricks together and without it the bricks would quickly crumble as they fatigued. This meant that the Israelites would now have to go and gather their own straw for the bricks, doubling their workload.

Once the Hebrews heard what Pharaoh had commissioned them concerning their daily quota of bricks and the lack of straw to produce them, they went murmuring to Moses and Aaron, saying, "Let the Lord look on you and judge, because you have made us abhorrent in the sight of Pharaoh and in the sight of his servants, to put the sword in their hand to kill us" (Ex. 5:21). After hearing these murmurings, Moses went three days out of Egypt and sacrificed to the Lord. The Lord again told Moses to go back to his people to let them know that the time had come for them to be taken out of Egypt, by God's Mighty Hand.

Moses' next encounter with Pharaoh will be the most remembered through all of the historical records of the Bible. When Aaron cast down the rod of Moses at the feet of Pharaoh, it transformed into a snake. Then Pharaoh commanded his magicians to do the same. As they cast their rods to the ground, turning them into snakes, Aaron's rod swallowed up the other rods. "And Pharaoh's heart grew hard, and he did not heed them, as the Lord said" (Ex. 7:13).

It is the Lord who keeps hardening the Pharaoh's heart so He, the Lord, can keep doing His great works in Egypt. Paul wrote this in Romans 9:18 concerning God's will: "Therefore He has mercy on whom He wills, and whom He wills He hardens". He has the ability to harden and soften the hearts of men and does this thing to fulfill His purpose.

The Ten Plagues:

Moses and Aaron would come before Pharaoh many more times and with many plagues before Pharaoh would relent to the will of their God. The following ten plagues that came upon Pharaoh's people come from Exodus 7:14 through 12:30).

>   First: Water of the Nile River turns to blood
>   Second: Frogs come upon the land
>   Third: Lie afflict man and beast

Fourth: Flies come upon the Egyptians
Fifth: Disease comes upon the livestock
Sixth: Boils break out on both man and beast
Seventh: Hail and fire
Eighth: Locusts devour crops and trees
Ninth: Darkness upon the land of Egypt
Tenth: Death to Egypt's first born

The tenth and final plague crushed Pharaoh and his people by taking the lives of their first-born children. Even Pharaoh's son who sat on his throne was taken from him.

The Exodus:

"Then he [Pharaoh] called for Moses and Aaron by night, and said, 'Rise, go out from among my people, both you and the children of Israel, and go, serve as you have said. Also take your flocks and your herbs, as you have said, and be gone; and bless me also'" (12:31-32).

It is also written that the Lord had given His people favor in the eyes of their former captors and whatever the Israelites asked of the Egyptians, whether it be silver, gold, or articles of clothing, it was given to them by the Egyptians.

As Moses led the twelve tribes of Israel out of Egypt, the Lord went before them in a pillar of cloud during the day and a pillar of fire by night to give them light. And it was as they were in the wilderness that the pillar of God led the Israelites to the edge of the Red (Reed) Sea and the children of Israel camped against the banks.

The Lord hardened Pharaoh's heart again against the Hebrew people, and Pharaoh set out with six hundred chariots and pursued the Israelites as far as the Red Sea. When the Israelites saw the chariots of the Pharaoh, they began to murmur and a cry out in terror to Moses.

The Lord said to Moses, "Why do you cry to Me? Tell the children of Israel to go forward" and "But lift up your rod, and stretch out your hand over the sea and divide it. And the children of Israel shall go on dry ground through the midst of the sea" (Ex. 14:15 – 16).

So the Lord caused the waters of the sea to divide and Moses and the Israelites passed through the midst of the sea on dry land. As the Egyptians pursued the Israelites through the divided waters, Moses lifted up his hand and passed it over the sea. The waters returned, drowning the Egyptians. This was the Lord's final battle with Pharaoh regarding the Israelites' flight from Egypt (The Sea Divided: Exodus, chapter 14).

The Israelites traveled three months before they reached Mount Sinai, where Moses received the "Ten Commandments" to give to the children of Israel. These tablets that contained the Ten Commandments were written by the finger of God. At one point, however, they had to be replaced because the children of Israel rose up to play and committed fornications against God while Moses was in the presence of God. The people, fearing Moses dead, commissioned Aaron to make for them a Golden Calf to lead them back to the Egyptians. Discovering their fornications, Moses came down from the mountain and smashed the tablets before the Israelites, took the calf, ground it into powder, and forced the Israelites to ingest it in their water. Nonetheless, the tablets were restored to the people and the people made way to the Promise Land.

As the people wandered through the wilderness of the Sinai, they constructed a tabernacle of animal skins to house the Ark of the Covenant—

A time came when Moses commissioned spies to go into the land of Canaan and bring back news of its inhabitants that they may go up and take the land from them. But when the spies returned to the people after forty days in Canaan, they brought back reports of mighty walled cities and peoples, even of giants who possessed the land. These reports scared the Israelites and again they murmured against the Lord and were too afraid to go up into Canaan. Again the people rejected God's word and the Lord became angry with the people. Moses went before God to intercede for the people.

The Lord rejected that evil generation that walked out of Egypt by His mighty hand. Except for Joshua, the son of Jephunneh, that generation would not enter the Promised Land but instead fall in the desert for forty years until they were no more. "But as for you, your carcasses shall fall [die] in this wilderness. And your sons shall be shepherds in the wilderness forty years, and bear brunt of your infidelity, until your carcasses are consumed in the wilderness" (Num. 14:32 – 33).

In the forty years that the Israelites dwelt in the wilderness, they came to see many signs and wonders of the Lord: The Manna from heaven (which they ate for forty years); the waters that came forth from the rock; the healing of snakebites; the bitter waters made sweet; and many other marvelous things done in their sights. Finally, the time came for Israel to cross over the Jordan and claim their inheritance from the Canaanite people.

At this time, Moses was one hundred twenty years old when he went out to speak to the people saying, "...I can no longer go out and come in. Also the Lord has said to me, 'You shall not cross over this Jordan'". Then Moses called Joshua and said to him in the sight of Israel, "Be strong and of good courage, for you must go with this people to the land which the Lord has sworn to their fathers to give them and you shall cause then to inherit it". And the Lord, He is the one who goes before you. He will be with you, He will not leave you nor forsake you; do not fear nor be dismayed" (Num. 31: 2-3; 7-8).

The Lord took Moses up to the top of Mount Nebo, and showed him all the land across the Jordan, which His children Israel will inherit. Then Moses was no more and the Lord hid his body on Mount Nebo in an unmarked grave. He was one hundred twenty at the time of his death. His death and the crossing of the Jordan into the Promised Land by Joshua and the Israelites both occurred about the year 1410 BC.

Joshua's first conquest in the land of Canaan is still his most memorable because the Lord had caused the walls of the city of Jericho to fall in the presence of Israel and their fame went all through the land of Canaan. Joshua conquered thirty-one kings in all in the land of Canaan, and he divided all the conquered lands between the twelve tribes of Israel. He died at the age of one hundred ten years old. After Joshua had died, new saviors would rise from the people and lead the Israelites until the time of the kings. These who rose between the death of Joshua and the time of Israel's first king, Saul, were called "judges". The judges spanned nearly four centuries, from about the fourteenth century BC to the eleventh century BC. Included among the many judges of Israel, and maybe one of the most famous of all the characters of the Bible, is Samson. We will explore this great savior of Israel's life and times in the next chapter.

Before I close this chapter, I would like to exhort all you readers to take time in these next months to study these first five books of the Bible (the Torah), from Genesis to Deuteronomy. The stories of Israel's sufferings and shortcomings can only be truly experienced by the process of in-depth study. I would like to take this time again to remind you that my thesis on Creation is to expose a biblical timeline regarding dates leading to the end times. The intent of my writing it not to paint any type of picturesque portraits of the biblical record, but just to simply place its contents in their appropriate chronological order according to the Lord's fifteen-day calendar of Creation.

Chapter 9

The Judges:

Joshua's conquest of the Promised Land began about the year 1410 BC and Joshua defeated thirty-one kings in all. Despite Joshua's attempt to purge the land of Canaan of all its inhabitants, thorns (Canaanites) were left in the lands with their gods, hindering Israel and testing the children of God. "Therefore I also said, 'I will not drive them out before you; but they shall be thorns in your side, and their gods shall be a snare to you'" (Judg. 2:3).

The Lord knew the hearts of the Israelites, His children, that they go easily astray to other peoples and to other gods. These were a people, in the times of the judges, just as we are today, who cannot seem to take control of their own individual circumstances and spiritual well-being. "In those days there was no king of Israel; everyone did what was right in his own eyes" (Judg. 21: 25).

Does this same analogy not apply to us today, that we seem to do what is right in our own eyes, forsaking even God's word? We often seem to care for the carnal and not the spiritual. Why do you think Israel strayed so quickly to foreign gods? This is because part of the worship processes of these other gods' involved sexual intercourse and other types of self-indulgences. Being born to the last generation of the second millennium myself (1961), I have seen with my own eyes the damaging self-indulgences of my generation. Open your eyes that have been blinded to these truths and you will see the plight that is consuming our self-reliant society of today.

Samson, the Atoning Savior of Israel:

The children of Israel again found themselves captives to the Philistines for forty years, at which time the Lord sent an angel to the wife of Manoah (of the tribe of Dan). "And the angel of the Lord appeared to the woman and said to her, 'Indeed now, you are barren and have borne no children, but you shall conceive and bear a son.' 'Now therefore, please be careful not to drink wine or similar drink, and not to eat anything unclean.' 'For behold, you shall conceive and bare a son. And no razor shall come upon his head, for the child shall be a Nazarite to God from the womb; and he shall begin to deliver Israel out of the hand of the Philistines'" (Judg. 13:3 – 5).

So the woman ran to her husband, Manoah, and told him all the man had told her. It also happened that the man (angel) came in the presence of Manoah and spoke to him, saying "Of all I said to the woman let her be careful...So the woman bore a son and called his name Samson; and the child grew, and the Lord blessed him" (Judg. 13:13, 24).

The angel of the Lord announced to the woman that her son would be a Nazarite to God. A Nazarite is one, either a man or woman, who vows to not drink wine or another product from the vine, or cut their hair until the period of time of their vow is completed. The length of the vow can vary from eight days to a lifetime. In Samson's case, his vow was from the womb until the time of his death.

Samson's Interaction with the Philistines:

Indeed Samson was a great warrior and champion of his people, but the lust of the eye would be a hindrance to him as he reigned as judge over his people. One day, as Samson traveled down to Timnah, he noticed a daughter of the Philistines and he was immediately smitten with her. He went and told his father and mother of the girl, but this displeased his parents because she was indeed a Philistine. After contending with his father and mother for a short time, Samson said to his father, "Get her for me, for she pleases me well". But his father and mother did not know that it was of the Lord—that He was seeking an occasion to move against the Philistines. For at that time, the Philistines had dominion over Israel (Judg. 14:3-4)

Samson again traveled down to Timnah, but this time with his father and mother to take the Philistine girl as his wife. When Samson came upon a vineyard in Timnah, a young lion attacked him. At that very moment, the Spirit of God came upon him and he tore the lion into pieces with his bare hands. He told no one of what had happened with the lion, however. Later, Samson returned to the lion's carcass and discovered that in the lion's carcass was a swarm of bees and a honeycomb. He took the honey and ate and gave some of the honey to his parents.

When the time of the wedding arrived, the Philistines brought thirty companions to be with him. Samson posed a riddle to them: "Out of the eater; came something to eat; and out of the strong; came something sweet" (v. 14). Samson gave the guests seven days to solve the riddle (the length of the wedding feast) or they would each have to bring him a garment of clothing. If they were able to solve his unsolvable riddle, Samson was to give to each of them a garment of clothing.

When the seventh day of the feast was upon them, the men went to Samson's wife in hopes that she might go to her husband to find the answer to his riddle. If she refused to help them, they threatened to burn her father's house down. She did as the Philistines asked and gave them the answer to the riddle. On the seventh day of the feast, the Philistines solved the riddle: "What is sweeter than honey? And what is stronger than a lion". And Samson, being angered with the men of the city said: "If you had not plowed with my heifer you would not have solved my riddle!" (v. 18).

Samson, in his anger, rose up and went down to Ashkelon and killed thirty Philistines, stripped them of their garments and brought them back to the thirty who solved the riddle. After this, he went back up to his father's house and his wife was given to a Philistine (his best man) who stood up for him at his wedding. A season had passed before Samson returned to Timnah to take his wife, but her father stopped Samson from entering into her chambers. He told Samson on that day that he had given his daughter to the Philistine. Samson, again angered, captured three hundred foxes, he tied them tail to tail, attached torches to their tails, and sent them running into the grain fields of the Philistines, burning their crops. The Philistines then went to his father-in-law's house and burnt both him and his daughter to death. Then Samson, following the death of his wife, began to slay the Philistines in great numbers. When he ceased killing he went down and dwelt in the clefts of Etam. And there the Philistines came against him. "He [Samson] found a fresh jawbone of a donkey, reached out his hand and took it, and killed a thousand men with it". "Then Samson said, 'With a jawbone of a donkey, heaps upon heaps, with the jawbone of a donkey I have slain a thousand men!'" (15: 15 – 16).

This would not be the last Philistine woman who would cause Samson to interact with the Philistines. "Afterward it happened that he loved a woman in the Valley of Sorek, whose name was Delilah" (Judg. 16:4).

Once the Philistine nobles found out the news of Samson's new love Delilah, they went to her with an offer to betray her lover Samson. Each man offered her eleven hundred pieces of silver. From that time forward, she sought to find the source of Samson's great strength to betray and give him into the hands of her people.

Three times Delilah had the Philistines lie in wait believing that Samson had revealed the secret of his strength to her and three times she tested Samson as he slept. The first was by binding him with seven fresh, undried bowstrings; the second by binding him with new ropes; and the third by weaving the seven locks of his hair into a web of a loom. Each time she tried to bind him, he quickly broke loose of constraints when awoken from his slumber. Following these three unsuccessful attempts to constrain him, Delilah said to him: "How can you say 'I love you', when your heart is not with me? You have mocked me these three times, and have not told me where your great strength lies" (16:15).

It was then that Samson revealed to Delilah the secret of his great strength, saying to her "No razor has ever come upon my head, for I have been a Nazarite to God from my mother's womb. If I am shaven, then my strength will leave me and I shall become weak, and be like any other man" (16:17). Believing that Samson was being truthful with her, she had the Philistines lie in wait the next time Samson came to her. Delilah lulled her lover to sleep and, as Samson slept, she called in one of her countrymen to shave the seven locks of hair from his head. Delilah screamed to the sleeping Samson, "The Philistines are upon you Samson!" But this time when he awoke, the Spirit of the Lord was not upon him, and the Philistines took him, blinded his eyes, and brought him down to Gaza. There they bound him with fetters of bronze and he became a grinder in the prison.

As time passed while Samson turned the great millstone that ground the grains of his Philistine captors, his seven locks of hair had grown back. This once-great champion of Israel, who slew thousands, was now again able to call upon the Spirit of God to strengthen him. But being blind and unable to navigate his way in or out of the hands of his captors, Samson would have to wait for an opportune time to deliver that one final blow upon his captors, the Philistines.

It was not long before such an opportunity presented itself. The Philistines would have great gatherings in the temple of their god Dagon. At these gatherings they would sacrifice to Dagon and have great celebrations in his name.

On this one particular occasion, they sent for Samson, that he might entertain the Philistines as they celebrated their pagan god. When the crowds' enthusiasm towards their captive began to simmer, they stationed him among the great pillars of the temple, by the hand of a young boy. When Samson came near the great pillars of the temple he asked the boy to bring him to the pillars so he could lean against them. The temple was full to its capacity with about three thousand men and women gathered on its rooftop. "Then Samson called to the Lord, saying, 'O Lord God, remember me, I pray! Strengthen me, I pray, just this once, O God that I may with one blow take vengeance on the Philistines for my two eyes!'" (Judg. 16:28).

Samson took hold of the two main pillars that supported the temple, one on his right and one on his left. He cried out his last words: "Let me die with the Philistines!" With all his might, Samson pushed on those two pillars, and the temple came falling down on all the people of the Philistines, including their rulers and lords. On that day, Samson killed thousands and his people were no longer captives of the Philistines.

Samson reigned as judge over Israel for twenty years before his death in the temple. Despite his flaws, he was a great man of God. Samson is among an elite group of biblical heroes and saviors who fought, in the name of God, to protect and lead their people Israel out of the hands of their captors. Following the noble death of their savior, Samson, the people would find themselves neck-deep in various adversities.

Before the time of the kings, another great judge arose over the Hebrew people. His name was Samuel, the son of Elkanah, of the tribe of Ephraim. Samuel would be the last judge of Israel and the first prophet to the kings. God worked mightily through Samuel and through Samuel God spoke to his people Israel. Samuel judged over Israel until the time of his sons, Joel and Abijah, but Israel rejected his sons because they did not deal fairly with the people. And it was at this time that Israel asked for a king to be placed over them to rule and judge. The people said to Samuel, "'Look, you are old, and your sons do not walk in your ways. Now make us a king to judge us like all the other nations' But this thing displeased Samuel when they said, 'Give us a king to judge us'. So, Samuel prayed to the Lord" (1 Sam. 8: 5 – 6).

So, Samuel became the last judge of Israel, and a new misfortune was about to come upon the Israeli people. By the people rejecting Samuel, they also rejected God as being their king. Their rejection of the Most High would cost Israel dearly.

Chapter 10

David:

Israel's demand for a king was answered by God, and He chose Saul, the son of Kish, to be king over His children Israel. However, Saul was a son of Benjamin. It had been prophesied by Jacob, when he prayed over and blessed his twelve sons, that the line of the kings would come from his son Judah: "The scepter shall not depart from Judah, nor a lawgiver from between his feet" (Gen. 49:10). This particular blessing prophesied the coming Messiah as coming from the tribe of Judah. Jesus, Himself, testifies of this in Revelation 22:16, saying: "...I am the root and offspring of David, the Bright and Morning Star".

Why, then, did the Lord command Samuel to anoint Saul as king? I believe the reason to be because Saul was the people's king, which meant that He, the Lord, gave the people what they asked for. It is recorded that Saul was a handsome man and a head taller that the average Israel man of his day. This tall and good-looking Benjamite was probably a charismatic figure in his day. Unfortunately, he was not a man after God's own heart. Saul was a very self-righteous man doing what was better in his own eyes instead of the Lord's will for him.

A time had come when the Lord commanded Saul to go up against the Amalek and totally destroy its people and livestock so that nothing remained. Saul, however, did not heed the Lord's words to totally destroy all of Amalekites. Instead, he spared king Agag and the best of the Amelekites' livestock. This caused the Lord to regret placing Saul as king over His people. "Now the word of the Lord came to Samuel, saying, 'I greatly regret that I have set up Saul as king, for he has turned back from following Me, and has not performed My commandments'". It grieved Samuel, who cried out to the lord all night." (1 Sam. 15:10 - 11).

Following the Lord's command, Samuel went to the house of Jesse, a son of the tribe of Judah, who dwelt in Bethlehem. Jesse had eight sons, the youngest of whom was named David. David was a shepherd and keeper of his father Jesse's flocks. Samuel came to Jesse's house with a flask of oil believing that he was to anoint an elder son of Jesse as king, but he found out that the one he was to anoint was actually a ruddy-looking teenager, the least of all of Jesse's sons. "But the Lord said to Samuel, 'Do not look at his appearance or physical stature, because I have refused him. For the Lord does not see as man sees; for man looks at the outward appearance, but the Lord looks at the heart'" (1 Sam. 16:7).

Now seven of Jesse's sons were with Samuel, but none were chosen of the seven to be king. So, Samuel asked Jesse if these were all of his sons, and Jesse answered, "There remains yet the youngest..." Then Samuel said to Jesse, "Send and bring him". Jesse sent for this youngest, David. "...Now he was ruddy, with bright eyes, and good-looking. And the Lord said, 'Arise; anoint him; for this is the one'". Then Samuel took the horn of oil and anointed him in the midst of his brothers; and the Spirit of the Lord came upon David from that day forward..." (1 Sam. 16:12 - 13).

David was born about the year 1044 BC and would not become king until the year 1014 BC., making him thirty years old when he became king. Before becoming king, while he was still of a young age, David defeated the Philistines' champion Goliath, who is recorded to have stood six cubits (a height of about 9'6"). Goliath was believed to be the son of an angel because he was of such great stature. The children of Israel feared this Philistine champion, but David had no fear of this giant. When Saul heard of the things David had said, he called for him and David said to King Saul, "let no man's heart fail because of him; your servant will go and fight with the Philistine". Moreover, David said, "The Lord, who delivered me from the paw of the lion and from the paw of the bear, He will deliver me from the hand of the Philistine". Saul said to David, "Go, and the Lord be with you" (17:32, 37).

Saul tried to array David in his armor but David was smaller in stature than the king. David took his staff in hand and his sling (the weapon of a shepherd), picked five smooth stones from the brook, and went out to the Philistine. David placed one of those smooth stones in his sling and shot it at the giant. The stone struck Goliath in the forehead, killing him, and David took the Philistine's sword out of its sheath and cut the giant's head off with it. When the Philistine army saw their champion dead at the hands of this ruddy boy, they took flight and the Israelites pursued them, killing many on that day. David became a mighty warrior in Saul's army and slew many Philistines. David was a great hero among his people and the Israel women sang of his victories:

"Saul has slain his thousands,
And David his ten thousand."

However, these chants for David were displeasing to Saul because he saw that the people loved David and favored him more than himself. And Saul said this in a flare of anger: "...Now what more can he have but the kingdom?"

From that time on Saul sought to destroy David, but David was beloved by all of Israel, so Saul was careful with his plot of David's demise. David eventually won the favor of Saul's daughter, Michal. He married her, the dowry that was asked for by Saul, for her hand in marriage, was one hundred foreskins of the Philistines. David delivered the one hundred foreskins and Michal was given to him as his wife. David was now as a prince in the house of Saul. Nonetheless, Saul still was displeased with David.

David and Jonathan, Saul's eldest son and heir to his throne, shared a profound brotherly love for one another. This was again displeasing to Saul because he feared for

Jonathan and his stake to the throne. Saul tried several times to take David's life, but each attempt would be yet another failure for the indelicate king. Because of Saul's relentless unresolved concerning David, David was forced to live as a refugee among his enemies.

A time came following Samuel's death that the Philistines were coming up against Saul. Saul gathered all the armies of Israel together and they encamped at Gilboa. Saul was now out of favor with God and, with Samuel dead, Saul had no one to bring word from the Lord. When Saul received no word from the Lord neither by dream nor prophet, he went to consult a medium in the land of En Dor. He hoped that the medium could awaken Samuel for him so that Samuel could tell him the outcome of this battle. The medium was able to awaken Samuel from his sleep and Samuel came up from Hades wearing a white mantel.

"Now Samuel said to Saul, 'Why have you disturbed me by bringing me up?' And Saul began to tell Samuel of the Philistines and that God has sent no word to him, and Samuel replied, 'And the Lord has done for Himself as He spoke by me. For the Lord has torn the kingdom out of your hand and given it to your neighbor, David'. Moreover the Lord will also deliver Israel with you into the hand of the Philistines. And tomorrow you and your sons will be with me [in Hades]. The Lord will also deliver the army of Israel into the hand of the Philistines" (1 Sam. 28:17, 19).

Even in his death, Samuel prophesied doom over Saul and his sons. As Samuel had told Saul, he and his sons, Jonathan, Abinadad, and Malchishua, were killed on the battlefield. Following Saul's death, David traveled to Hebron with his two wives and his men and their families, where they settled in the cities of Hebron. "Then the men of Judah came, and there they anointed David king over the house of Judah. And they told David, saying, 'The men of Jebesh Gilead were the ones who buried Saul'" (2 Sam. 2:4). David reigned seven and a half years in Hebron before he became king of all Israel. After this, he reigned thirty-three years in

Jerusalem, until the time of his death at the age of seventy years old.

David began his reign in Jerusalem about the year 1007 BC. At one point, Israel was at war with the Ammonites. David, while Israel was in battle, came out to the roof of his house one evening and saw a woman bathing on her rooftop. The woman was very beautiful and David grew wanton towards her. So, David sent for the woman, whose name was Bathsheba, and lay with her. She became pregnant with his child. Unfortunately, Bathsheba was a married woman, the wife of Uriah the Hittite, who was in battle against the Ammonites. David sent for Uriah, hoping that he would take leave from the battle and lay with his wife. But Uriah, being loyal to his fellow soldiers in battle, would not go lie with his wife, Bathsheba. When David found this out, he sent Uriah back into battle with a letter to Joab, his commander. "And he wrote in the letter, saying, 'Set Uriah in the forefront of the hottest battle, and retreat from him, that he may be struck down and die'" (2 Sam. 11:15).

This was a terrible betrayal against Uriah, David's servant, and the Lord's anger was hot against David. The Lord sent Nathan the prophet to David with a parable concerning this evil he committed against His Commandments. Once David heard the parable and realized that it was meant for him, he fell to his knees. "So David said to Nathan, 'I have sinned against the Lord'. And Nathan said to David, 'The Lord also has put away your sin; you shall not surely die'. 'However, because by this deed you have given great occasion to the enemies of the Lord to blaspheme, the child also who is born to you shall surely die'" (2 Sam. 13 - 14). As Nathan had said, Bathsheba's child lived only a short time–seven days. For the entire seven days of his life, his father David fasted while pleading with the Lord to spare his life. Even with the unfortunate death of her first child, Bathsheba would bare other sons to David–Solomon (who would become king), Nathan (whose descendants would bring forth the Messiah), Shimea, and Shobab.

David had many sons. The oldest, Amnon, would be murdered by his brother Absalom regarding the rape of his sister Tamar. Absalom was also murdered, in battle when he tried to overthrow his father David. Through all this sorrow that would befall David, it would be Solomon who would become king over Israel.

While David reigned in Jerusalem, he wanted to build a house to the Lord, but his request was denied by God because of the blood on his hands. However, the Lord did promise David this: "When your days are fulfilled and you rest with your fathers, I will set up your seed after you, who will come from your body, and I will establish his kingdom'...'He shall build a house for My name, and I will establish the throne of his kingdom forever'" (2 Sam. 7:12 - 13).

So, this great task of building a house to the Lord in Jerusalem fell to David's son Solomon, who became well known for his wisdom. It is recorded in the Bible that the queen of Sheba came to hear the words of Solomon, and, upon hearing and seeing the great accomplishments of this man, she said this: "Happy are your men and happy are these servants, who stand continually before you and hear your wisdom!' 'Blessed be the Lord your God, who delighted in you, setting you on the throne of Israel! Because the Lord has loved Israel forever, therefore He made you king, to do justice and righteousness'" (1 Kgs. 10:8 - 9).

The Temple Mount:

"And it came to pass in the four hundred and eightieth year after the children of Israel had come out of the land of Egypt, in the fourth year of Solomon's reign over Israel, in the month of Ziv, which is the second month, that he began to build the house of the Lord" (1 Kgs. 6:1). Solomon began the construction of the temple about the year 970 BC and completed it about the year 963 BC (approximately seven years).

Solomon reigned forty years over Israel, and in that time period, he gained for himself much wealth. It is also recorded in 1 Kings 11:1 - 13 that Solomon also gained seven hundred wives (princesses) and three hundred concubines, These women came from many kingdoms and with them came many of their gods. Solomon would eventually stray from the Lord, in his old age, and begin to worship some of the gods of his wives and concubines. Solomon angered the Lord with his idolatries. "Therefore the Lord said to Solomon, 'Because you have done this, and have not kept My covenant and My statutes, which I have commanded you, I will surely tear the kingdom away from you and give it to your servant'. 'Nevertheless I will not do it in your days, for the sake of your father David; I will tear it out of the hand of your son'. However I will not tear away the whole kingdom; I will give one tribe to your son for the sake of My servant David, and for the sake of Jerusalem which I have chosen'" (vv. 11 - 13).

On the day of Solomon's death, about the year 934 BC, Rehoboam became king of Israel. However, as it was said by the word of the Lord, the kingdom was torn from his hand. David reigned over the whole of Israel for thirty-three years. Solomon reigned over Israel for forty years. Now, the northern kingdom was given to Jeroboam, the son of Nebat, to reign as king. The ten northern tribes of Israel would never again be one with the tribes of Judah and Benjamin. These ten northern tribes would eventually be scattered through the lands of their captor Assyria. Today, they have come to be known as the lost tribes of Israel.

Rehoboam reigned over the tribes of Judah and Benjamin for seventeen years, and there was war between him and Jeroboam throughout his entire reign.

During the reigns of the kings of Judah and Israel many prophets of God came with their messages of doom to their defiant and rebellious kings. One of these kings, Ahab, took for a wife Jezebel, the daughter of Ethball (king of Sidon). Ahab began to worship Baal (a pagan deity). "Then he set up an alter for Baal in the temple of Baal, which he had built in Samaria" (1 Kgs. 16:32).

Ahab did much evil in the sight of God and, in his days, came a great prophet named Elijah. The prophet came to Ahab, saying, "As the Lord God of Israel lives, before whom I stand, there shall not be dew nor rain these years, except by my word" (17:1). And by the word of the Lord, given to Elijah, no rain fell on Israel for three and a half years. Israel was cursed with no rain because of this king's idolatries and the wickedness of his wife's fornications with Baal. Jezebel would come to massacre the prophets of God to place her prophets of Baal over the people of Israel. Elijah, the prophet of God, however, would come to do battle with the prophets of Baal. One of Elijah's great battles with the prophets of Jezebel was on Mount Carmel, where he slew four hundred fifty prophets in one day. This massacre of Jezebel's prophets would provoke her now to seek Elijah's life. "Then Jezebel sent a messenger to Elijah, saying, 'So let the gods do to me, and more also, if I do not make your life as the life of one of them by tomorrow about this time" (1 Kgs. 19:2). It's recorded that after Elijah received this message from Jezebel that he fled to Horeb and hid himself in a cave, waiting to hear from God.

Elijah survived Jezebel's threat and, after a time passed, went to Ahab with this disturbing message from the Lord: "And concerning Jezebel the Lord also spoke, saying, 'The dogs shall eat Jezebel by the wall of Jezreel'...'The dogs shall eat whoever belongs to Ahab and dies in the city, and the birds of the air shall eat whoever dies in the field'. But there was no one like Ahab who sold himself to do wickedness in the sight of the Lord, because Jezebel his wife stirred him up" (1 Kgs. 21:23 - 25).

It came to pass as the Lord had said. Ahab died in battle and the dogs licked up his blood that dripped from his chariot, and Jezebel his wife was thrown from the window of the wall of Jezreel. Her blood spattered on the wall and on the horse as she was trampled. When they returned to retrieve Jezebel's body, they found: "...the skull and the feet and the palms of her hands" (2 Kgs. 9:35). For the dogs had eaten her as prophesied by Elijah to her husband Ahab. And, according to the prophecy, there would be no burial place for Jezebel in Israel.

Elijah Taken Up to Heaven:

Before the death of this wicked seductress Jezebel, Elijah was taken up into heaven in the witness of his disciple Elisha. As Elijah and Elisha came to the edge of the river Jordan, "...Elijah took his mantle [cloak], rolled it up and struck the water; and it was divided this way and that, so that the two of them crossed over on dry land" (2 Kgs. 2:8).

Elijah's mantle was anointed with power, as was Moses' rod, and, as Moses' rod brought forth miracle upon miracle, Elijah's mantle did the same. "And so it was as they had crossed over, that Elijah said to Elisha, 'Ask! What may I do for you, before I am taken away from you?' Elisha said, 'Please let a double portion of your spirit be upon me'"..."Then it happened, as they continued on and talked, that suddenly a chariot of fire appeared with horses of fire, and separated the two of them; and Elijah went up by a whirlwind into heaven" (vv. 9, 11).

So it was as Elijah ascended up into Heaven by the whirlwind, he dropped his mantle and Elisha retrieved it. Doing as his master before him, he struck the waters of the Jordan and caused them to separate. Elisha crossed back over the Jordan on dry land with a double anointment from his master Elijah.

Jeremiah the Weeping Prophet:

In the time of Jehoiakim, son of Josiah, king of Judah, there was a prophet named Jeremiah who would warn the king of Judah's impending doom and captivity at the hands of Babylonian king Nebuchadnezzer, Needless to say, his warnings were not heeded and Judah fell into the hands of this pagan king.

Jeremiah is called the weeping prophet because of his many lamentations he made for his people. For forty years he proclaimed a message of doom and coming captivity in Babylon, but by this time in Judah's history, the people had grown stubborn and stiff-necked, caring nothing for the word of His prophets.

Chapter 11

Babylon:

In the first year of Nebuchadnezzar's reign, the Lord sent Jeremiah the prophet to the people of Judah, despite their refusal to repent, to give them yet another warning of the impending doom that was to befall them at the hands of Nebuchadnezzer, king of Babylon. "And this whole land shall be a desolation and an astonishment, and these nations shall serve the king of Babylon seventy years...'Then it will come to pass, when seventy years are completed, that I will punish the king of Babylon and the nation, the lands of the Chaldeans, for their iniquity,' says the Lord; 'and I will make it a perpetual desolation'" (Jer. 25:11 - 12).

Yet, again, upon hearing the word of God, the people of Judah did not repent. The prophecy came to be fulfilled. In the nine years of his reign, King Nebuchadnezzer besieged the city of Jerusalem and captured King Zedekiah, killing his sons before his eyes and then blinding him. The city walls were broken down and the temple was destroyed by fire. When the city was destroyed with the temple, Nebuchadnezzer had all the treasure of the city, including the artifacts from the temple taken to Babylon and stored in the king's treasury. Unfortunately, most of Judah's inhabitants also were taken to Babylon. For those left behind, however, the king set a governor in charge in Judah.

The historical record tells us that Nebuchadnezzer besieged Jerusalem in about the year 587 BC. However, my calculations based off of Daniel's "Seventy Week" prophecy reveal a different date, the year 521 BC.

Daniel was one of the captives who were taken to Babylon when Nebuchadnezzer besieged Jerusalem and destroyed its temple. Daniel was also a very gifted interpreter of dreams, just as Jacob's son Joseph (who interpreted Pharaoh's dreams and became governor over all of Egypt) had been. Daniel, too, would be raised up by Nebuchadnezzer to a position of governor over many of the territories of Babylon because of his ability to decipher dreams. It's recorded in Daniel chapter 2 that in the second year of Nebuchadnezzar's reign a dream came to him that was very troubling. So Nebuchadnezzer sent for all the wise men of his kingdom: the magicians, astrologers, soothsayers, and the like—to not only interpret his dream, but they would also have to have the dream revealed to then through their own mystical understandings. I believe the king did this to his subjects to test them and truly find the wisest man of all his kingdom.

When no one was able to receive and decipher the king's dreams, Nebuchadnezzer put out a decree to kill all the wise men of the kingdom. This decree would also include killing Daniel and his companions. One night, however, as Daniel lay his head on his pillow, the dream was revealed to him and its interpretation. Daniel rose up and went to Arioch, who the king had put in charge of killing the wise men. Arioch brought Daniel before the king and Daniel revealed the dream and its interpretations to the king: "'You, O king, were watching; and behold, a great image! This great image, whose splendor was excellent, stood before you; and its form was awesome". This image's head was of fine gold, its chest and arms of silver, its belly and thighs of bronze, "its legs of iron, its feet partly of iron and partly of clay" (vv. 31 – 33).

Daniel went on to tell the king the remainder of his dream. Daniel told the king that he saw a stone that was cut without hands and crushed the statue's feet and broke them into pieces. The head of gold, the chest of silver, and the thighs of bronze were crushed together and made like chaff of the threshing floor. Daniel said that the wind blew away the chaff until it was gone. Daniel had now interpreted Nebuchadnezzar's dream, revealing that the king was the head of gold and that three inferior kingdoms were to follow after his.

One of the three coming kingdoms that were revealed to Daniel in this dream that would come to follow Nebuchadnezzar's was the Medes and Persians. This was to be the kingdom of silver. The second kingdom, the kingdom of bronze, would follow the Persians. It would be called Greece. The third kingdom to follow Nebuchadnezzer, and the fiercest of all the kingdoms before it would be Rome. This is the kingdom of iron partly mixed with clay. This dream would only be one of many that Daniel would receive and interpret concerning these coming kingdoms and their kings.

In the first year of Belshazzar (about the year 489 BC), when Nebuchadnezzar's grandson reigned, Daniel again had a dream vision concerning these four kingdoms. In it the kingdoms were animals. One was a lion, the second a bear, the third a leopard (which had four heads), and the fourth he described in this manner: "After this I saw in the night visions, and behold, a fourth beast, dreadful and terrible, exceedingly strong, it had huge iron teeth; it was devouring, breaking in pieces, and trampling the residue with its feet. It was different from all the beasts that were before it, and it had ten horns...I was considering the horns, and there was another horn, a little one, coming up among them, before whom three of the first horns were plucked out by the roots, And there, in this horn, were eyes like the eyes of a man, and a mouth speaking pompous words" (7:7 - 8)

This fourth beast, again, is the Roman Empire. It is not, however, the Romans who conquered Greece in approximately the year 150 BC when Rome was still a Republic. This fourth beast of Daniel sprouted its first horn about the year 27 BC, when Octavian, the nephew of Julius Caesar, became the first Emperor of Rome. After Octavian (Augustus Caesar), four other horns would sprout. The fourth horn that sprouted from Octavian (i.e. the fifth horn of the beast) would be considered an abomination to the children of Israel, Daniel's people. This fifth horn is Nero.

In the first year of Darius I, king of the Chaldeans (which was approximately the year 451 BC, according to biblical record), Daniel began praying and fasting regarding Judah's seventy-year captivity and what would be the sign of the end. Gabriel, one of the chief angels, came to Daniel to reveal what would take place concerning his people. These are the words that Gabriel spoke to Daniel: "Seventy weeks are determined for your people and for your holy city, to finish the transgression, to make an end of sins, to make reconciliation for iniquity, to bring in everlasting righteousness, to seal up vision and prophecy, and to anoint the Most High [Christ Jesus] "...know therefore and understand, that from the going forth of the command to restore and build Jerusalem until Messiah the Prince, there shall be seven weeks and sixty-two weeks; the street shall be built again and the wall, even in troublesome times...And after the sixty-two weeks Messiah shall be cut off [crucified], but not for himself; and the prince [Nero] who is to come shall destroy the city and the sanctuary, The end of it shall be with a flood, and till the end of the war desolations are determined. Then he shall confirm a covenant with many for one week; but in the middle of the week he shall bring an end to sacrifice and offering. And on a wing of abominations shall be one who makes desolation, even until the consummation, which is determined, is poured out on the desolate" (Dan 9:24 - 27).

These seventy weeks that were determined for the people began when King Darius reaffirmed a decree that was sent out by Cyrus the Great in the first year of his reign (about the year 473 BC). However, when Zerubbel, who was of the lineage of David, went to Jerusalem, he came across much opposition. The building of the temple and its walls were delayed. In the first year of Darius, however, the building of the temple resumed, and by the sixth year of his reign the temple was completed. This would have been about the year 445 BC, as recorded in the book of Ezra: "Now the temple was finished on the third day of the month of Adar, which was in the sixth year of the reign of King Darius" (6:15). Upon completion of the temple by Zerubbel in the year 445 BC, Nehemiah would not complete the rebuilding of the walls of Jerusalem until about the year 402 BC (about seventy years following the first decree from King Cyrus).

Then it was determined that sixty-two weeks would pass before Messiah was crucified, which would have been about the year 32 AD. This is what ends the first sixty-nine weeks of Daniel's seventy-week prophecy. (All the dates of this prophecy are derived from the Julian Calendar).

The seventieth week of Daniel's prophecy would prove to be the most devastating for Daniel's people. In this week (group of seven years), the city of Jerusalem would be besieged by the Romans, the temple destroyed and the people disbursed throughout the Roman Empire. It would be the emperor Nero who would cause the wall to tumble down on the Jewish people. As Gabriel told Daniel in this prophecy that "seventy weeks are determined for your people and the holy city". This means that at the end of the seventieth week, the city would be made desolate and its people (the Jews) disbursed into the empire of its conqueror, the Romans, in about the year 70 AD.

In Daniel chapter 8, a vision is recorded concerning this little horn that is to bring desolation upon the holy city and its people.

The Vision of the Ram and the Goat:

Daniel reveals in this vision that he saw a ram with two horns, one more prominent then that other, that pushed westward, northward, and southward, and no other beast could stop it. Then, as he is considering what he had just seen, another beast appears. It is a male goat with one horn on its head who came from the west and never touched the ground as it crossed the surface of the whole earth. When the goat came to the ram, he attacked him with furious power, breaking its two horns and trampling the ram into the ground. There was no one on the entire earth who could deliver the ram from the goat's power. "Therefore the male goat grew very great; but when he became strong, the large horn was broken, and four noble ones came up toward the four winds of heaven" (v. 8).

In verses 15 – 27, Daniel gives the interpretation of his vision, which was revealed to him by the angel Gabriel. It is recorded in verse 21 that the male goat is the kingdom of Greece and the horn on its head is its first king, Alexander the Great. Alexander was born about the year 356 BC, the son of King Philip II, who was assassinated about the year 336 BC. Alexander took the throne at the age of twenty and unified the Greek people. About the year 330 BC, Alexander defeated Darius III, king of the Persians and extended his empire from Greece to India. However, he did not live a very long life. He died at the age of thirty-three, in about the year 323 BC.

The four horns represented four generals who served under Alexander at the time of his death. Alexander died leaving no true heir to his throne, so, by the year 306 BC, Antigonus, Craterus, Ptolemy, and Seleucus divided the kingdom into four separate empires: the Antigonid Empire; the Selecid Empire; the Bactrian Empire; and the Ptolemic Empire. As it was written by Daniel in verse 22, "...Four kingdoms shall arise out of that nation, but not with its power."

The Little Horn:

"And out of one of them came a little horn which was exceedingly great towards the south, towards the east, and towards the Glorious Land. And it grew up to the host of heaven; and it cast down some of the host and some of the stars to the ground, and trampled them. He even exalted himself as high as the prince of host; and by him the daily sacrifices were taken away, and the place of His sanctuary was cast down [The Temple]" (vv. 9 - 11).

You may suppose that this little horn, which came out from one of the four noble horns, would be Greek. However, when we revisit Daniel's vision of the "Four Beasts" in chapter 7, we see that this little horn came out of the fourth beast, Rome (vv. 7 - 8). Greece was the third beast described in verse 6: "After I looked, and there was another, like a leopard, which had on its back four wings of a bird. The beast also had four heads, and domain was given to it". The four wings and the four heads of the leopard represent the kingdom being divided into four parts with four separate Emperors. This leopard of Daniel 7:6 is swallowed up by this fourth beast, Rome, about the year 150 BC, according to the Julian Calendar. Once Greece was conquered by the Romans, the Greeks never rose up in power again regarding world conquest.

From the time of Alexander's death in 323 BC until the time that Greece was conquered by the Romans in 150 BC, the Greek culture was still dominate throughout the known world. This was, and still is, called the Hellenistic Period. During the time of Judas Maccabeus, on December 25, 168 BC, the Hellenists set up an altar to their god Zeus in the temple at Jerusalem. This began a revolt led by Judas Maccabeus that lasted about three years. Maccabeus succeeded in driving out the Hellenists and cleansing the temple by the year 165 BC. The "Altar of Zeus" was referred to as the "Abomination of Desolation" recorded in Daniel's seventy-week prophecy. However, this particular profane act against the Lord and the Jewish people did not cause the end of sacrifice and offerings that Daniel prophesied in verse 27. In fact, it helped to strengthen the Jewish people for a short period of time.

It was the little horn, a ruler who was to come out of the fourth beast that would bring an end to the Jewish people's way of worship and offerings. "He even exalted himself as high as the Prince of host [Christ Jesus]; and by him the daily sacrifices were taken away, and the place of His [the Lord's] sanctuary was cast down" (Dan. 8:11).

It is recorded that in approximately the year 66 AD, Nero, then emperor, placed a statue in the temple at Jerusalem of himself to be worshipped as a god. This would cause the Great Revolt. Again the Jews rose up against their oppressors, the Romans, causing war to come upon the city of Jerusalem for about three and a half years. In the year 70 AD, Titus, the son of Vespasian, emperor of Rome, with his legions destroyed the temple and the city. Vespasian had all the Jews of Palestine disbursed throughout his empire.

Daniel's vision of the ram and goat, concerning the four noble horns and the little horn that comes forth from one of the noble horns, has several different interpretations. The first interpretation, given by Gabriel in Daniel 8:15 - 27, is regarding the kingdom of Greece and its kings who were to come. Its second interpretation can also apply to Julius Caesar, being the broken horn, and the line of emperor of Rome who would follow him. The four noble horns were: Octavian (Augustus Caesar), who ruled Rome from 27 BC to 14 AD; Tiberius, who reigned from 14 AD to 37 AD; Caligula, who reigned as emperor from 37 AD to 41 AD; and Claudius Caesar (believed to have been poisoned by Nero's mother), who reigned from 41 AD to 54 AD. The little horn, "having fierce features, who understands sinister schemes" is Nero.

If we were to consider either Alexander or Julius Caesar as the broken horn and either the four generals of Greece or the four emperors of Rome as the four noble horns, both interpretations lead to the same little horn, Nero. However, our last and final interpretation of this broken horn and its four noble horns will bring forth a ruler unlike the world has ever seen since the beginning of man. He will be a very sinister and vile man, caring for nothing but his power and conquest of the world.

We will revisit this vision at a later time, revealing the little horn of Daniel chapter 7:8.

Chapter 12

The Roman Empire:

According to the Sicilian historian Timaeus, who lived around the year 300 BC, the City of Rome was founded about the year 814 BC. For nearly three hundred years, Rome was ruled under a monarchal system of government. In about the year 509 BC, the last Roman king was overthrown and the Republic of Rome was born. It was under the Republic (two-party system) that Rome began to unify Italy. In about the year 264 BC, Rome emerged as the strongest power of the Mediterranean region. The Republic grew and the Senate's power grew along with it. The Senate came to be the chief policy-making body of the Roman state.

One of the most famous men that would emerge from the Roman Republic was Gaius Julius Caesar. Caesar was born on July 12, 100 BC. He would rise to power through the political ambitions of his family and would eventually become proconsul of Gaul, and then dictator of Rome; following his defeat over Pompey the Great. Caesar was also well known for his affair with the enchanting Cleopatra, whose rule over Egypt he would solidify by defeating her brother Ptolemy XIII in battle.

In the year 46 BC, Caesar reformed the Roman calendar. The original yearly Roman calendar consisted of 360 days and was commonly incorrect regarding the beginning of the seasons. The original calendar was inaccurate concerning any type of predictable yearly events. So Caesar added five and one quarter days to the calendar, with a "leap year" every four years (which consisted of 366 days).

The Julian calendar was used from the year 46 BC to the year 1582 AD, a total of 1,628 years. In the year 1628 of the

Julian calendar, a Roman monk named Dionysius Exiguus determined that the Julian calendar year was eleven minutes and fourteen seconds too long. He discovered that this caused the calendar to be skewed by ten days from when it was first revised in 46 BC. Dionysius corrected the error and began to calculate the birth of the Messiah, Jesus of Nazareth.

The original Roman calendar has been traced back to about the year 752 BC. This 360-day calendar went virtually unrevised for 706 years, which meant that, even though it was a lunar calendar, it may have been off by close to ten years. The Jewish lunar calendar added a thirteenth month every seven years to help keep it aligned with the seasons. Caesar's calendar of 365 ¼ days and a leap year of 366 days was able to keep the calendar in balance with the seasons.

Dionysius introduced the concept of numbering years through a system of fourteen different calendars. This new system would be the creation of our modern-day calendar (the Gregorian calendar), which still consists of 365 ¼ days and the leap year as the Julian calendar, still in use today, which gives us a very close approximation of our Savior's birth. BC is an abbreviation for "Before Christ". Another commonly used abbreviation to refer to the years before Christ is BCE, meaning "Before the Christian Era". According to the Roman calendar, 1 BC corresponds to the year 752, and the year of Christ's birth (1 AD) corresponds to the year 753. Ad is an abbreviation of the Latin words "Anno Domini" its translated meaning is "the day of the Lord".

The question is how did Dionysius come to derive this date that we determine to be the year of our Lord, or the birth of Christ?

The answer lies in our Bible. According to Luke 2:1, Caesar Augustus sent out a decree throughout the empire that the entire world should be registered. This census of the Jewish people would cause Joseph and Mary to travel to Bethlehem, the city of David, to register. This was because Joseph was of the house of David and would have to register in Bethlehem. When Mary and Joseph reached Bethlehem, Mary gave birth to Jesus.

Augustus reigned from the year 725 to the year 766, according to the years of the Roman calendar. These would be the years 27 BC to 14 BC of our modern-day calendar. This, on its own, would not nearly be enough information to conclude any particular date. However, in Luke 3:1, it is recorded that Jesus began his ministry during the reign of Tiberius Caesar (the second emperor of Rome). "Now in the fifteenth year of the reign of Tiberius Caesar, Pontius Pilate being governor of Judea, and Herod being tetrarch of Galilee..."

Tiberius reigned from the years 766 to 789 of the Roman calendar. It is recorded in Luke 3:23, that Jesus was about thirty years old when he began his ministry. So, if we were to add fifteen years to the year 766, the beginning of Tiberius' reign, we would come to the year 781 of the Roman calendar. Going back about 29 years, assuming that Jesus may have been just on the cusp of his thirtieth birthday, we come to the date of 752 of the Roman calendar. This means that Jesus was born in the year 753 of the Roman calendar, which we now translate as 1 AD of our current calendar.

As I am writing this particular lesson, it is currently the year 2011. My belief is that our calendar of today is accurate within a year of Christ Jesus' birth. He may have been born anywhere between the years 1 BC and 1 AD. This is a close enough approximation of His birth regarding the prophecies of the Bible that are yet to come.

The Birth of the Beast:

"Then I stood on the sand of the sea. And I saw a beast rising out of the sea, having seven heads and ten horns, and on his horns ten crowns, and on his heads a blasphemous name." (Rev. 13:1).

This beast is the beast that will be upon the earth in the end times, when Christ will come with His angels to cleanse the earth from all unrighteousness. This is also the fourth beast of Daniel's prophecy recorded in chapter 7, verses 7 – 27. Daniel's beast has ten horns (representing ten kings), just as John the Revelator's beast reveals. However, Daniel's beast has only one head and John's has seven. Why? Unlike Daniel's single-headed beast, which represents the same kingdom or empire, John's seven-headed beast actually reveals the progression of the beast from its beginning to its destructive ending.

Rome is illustrated by both the beast of Daniel and John, just as Greece was also illustrated in both Daniel 7:6 (as a four-headed leopard, representing the four generals of Greece) and Daniel 8:8 (as a four-horned goat). Two separate beasts illustrating the same kingdom, revealing the progression and eventual collapse of the kingdom of Greece.

In approximately the year 44 BC, Julius Caesar was murdered at the hands of the Senate. The republic was in much need for reform and Caesar saw an opportunity to not only restructure the corrupt governmental system of the Senate, but also to exalt himself as king or emperor of the Roman Empire. This was unacceptable to the Senate, so they conspired to assassinate him. On March 15th of 44 BC, Brutus and Cassius (Roman Senators) stabbed Caesar to death while he attended a meeting in the Senate. Both Brutus and Cassius were tracked down and killed by Octavian, Caesar's nephew, and the famous Mark Anthony, the general of Rome who conspired with Cleopatra and went to war with his beloved Rome.

In the year 27 BC, Octavian became the first emperor of Rome and would now take the name Augustus Caesar. Augustus is well known in history for his defeat of Mark Anthony and Cleopatra in the year 30 BC. At the time of Julius Caesar's murder, the large horn of the goat prophesied by Daniel is broken. In the year 27 BC, the first of the four noble horns appeared, which corresponds to the first head of the seven-headed beast of Revelations 13:1. The year 27 BC would see the birth of the Roman Empire. As we progress through these writings, I will reveal the remaining six emperors or rulers represented by the beast, including those who have fallen and who are to come.

Chapter 13

The Birth of Messiah:

By the year 63 BC, the Romans entered Jerusalem and Judah quickly transformed it into a providence of Rome. By the year 37 BC, Herod the Great would become king of all Judea and an ally to the Senate. Herod would reign until his death in 4 AD. He would be proceeded by his sons, Herod, Philip, and Lysanias, tetrarch of Abilene. By 6 AD, Augustus Caesar was emperor of Rome and Jerusalem had come under direct Roman rule and was governed by the Roman procurators.

Gabriel's Announcement:

In the twenty-seventh year of the reign of Augustus, which would have been about the year 1 BC, the Lord sent Gabriel to Zacharias the priest to announce the birth of his son John. "And Zacharias said to the angel, 'How shall I know this? For I am an old man, and my wife is well advanced in years?' And the angel answered and said, 'I am Gabriel, who stands in the presence of God, and was sent to speak to you and bring you these glad tidings'" (Lk. 1:18-190. Because of Zacharias' doubt, Gabriel rendered him mute until the birth of his son. Elizabeth, Zacharias' wife, conceived as it was said by Gabriel.

Six months after Zacharias and Elizabeth's baby's conception, the Lord sent Gabriel to Mary, the betrothed of Joseph, the son of Heli, who was of the lineage of David. Mary, a cousin of Elizabeth, may have also been one of the daughters of Aaron (a Levite).

When Gabriel appeared to Mary, she was frightened, not knowing the reason for the visit. "Then the angel said to her, 'Do not be afraid, Mary, for you have found favor with God...And behold, you will conceive in your womb and bring forth a Son, and shall call His name Jesus. He will be great, and will be called the Son of the Most High; and the Lord God will give Him the throne of His father David...And He will reign over the house of Jacob forever, and of His kingdom there will be no end'. Then Mary said to the angel, 'How can this be, since I do not know a man?' And the angel answered to her, 'The Holy Spirit will come upon you, and the power of the Highest will overshadow you; therefore, also, that Holy One who is to be born will be called the Son of God.'" Then Gabriel announced to Mary that her cousin Elizabeth was also with child, and Mary went to Judah, from Galilee, to visit her cousin Elizabeth. And when Mary went into the house of Zacharias to visit Elizabeth (who was six-months pregnant), the baby leapt in Elizabeth's womb, and Elizabeth was filled with the Holy Spirit.

When Mary returned from her visit with Elizabeth in Judah, she would have to confront Joseph with the news of her conception. This must have been a very scary and uneasy time for Mary, trying to explain to the man who would be her future husband that she was now impregnated by the Lord Almighty. It is recorded in Matthew 1:18 – 25 that an angel of the Lord visited Joseph in a dream and revealed this mystery of Mary's conception to him, saying, "'Joseph, son of David, do not be afraid to take to you Mary your wife, for that which is conceived in her is of the Holy Spirit...And she will bring forth a Son, and you shall call His name Jesus, for He will save His people from their sins'...Then Joseph, being aroused from his sleep, did as the angel of the Lord commanded him and took to him his wife". (vv. 20 – 21, 24).

In the twenty-eighth year of Augustus' reign (which would have been the year 1 AD), he sent out a decree that all the world should be registered. This meant that Joseph, being of the house of David, would have to travel to

Bethlehem in Judah to register him and his family. So, Joseph sat Mary on a donkey and traveled to Nazareth to Bethlehem. Mary was in her ninth month of pregnancy at this time. I believe this was the month of Tishri, the beginning of the Jewish New Year, which falls between September and October of our modern-day calendar. "So it was, that while they were there, the days were completed for her to deliver Jesus. "And she brought forth her firstborn Son, and wrapped Him in swaddling clothes. And laid Him in a manger, because there was no room for them in the inn" (Lk. 2:6 – 7).

Jesus was born to the first generation of the fourth day of man, the twelfth millennium of the Lord's calendar of creation. This would mean that fifty generations have passed from Judah, the son of Jacob, to Joseph, the son of Heli. This completes another two thousand years of the Lord's millennial calendar. The two-thousand-year reign of the 12 patriarchs of Israel have come to a close. The reign of the 12 Apostles are about to be ushered in.

Both the gospels of Luke and Matthew mention Herod, the king of Judah. It is recorded in Matthew chapter 2, concerning the arrival of the wise men from the East, that upon their arrival, they spoke with Herod concerning the birth of the Messiah. History records Herod's reign from the years 37 BC until his death in 4 BC. This date of 4 BC does not conform to the timelines concerning both the reigns of Augustus and Tiberius in Luke's account of Jesus' conception and of the beginning year of Jesus' ministry at the age of thirty. If Herod did indeed die in the year 4 BC, Jesus would have to have been born somewhere between 10 and 7 BC. Why? Matthew's gospel indicates that the wise men arrived in Jerusalem about two years after the birth of Jesus: "...From two years old and under, according to the time which had been determined from the wise men" (Mt. 2:16). This discrepancy concerning the date of Herod's death and the birth of the Messiah is a clerical error—not a biblical one. It may be that Herod died in the year 4 AD and not in 4 BC. This new date would align perfectly with the biblical account.

When eight days had passed from Jesus' birth, he was circumcised in the custom of the Jewish people and brought under the Law. He was brought under the Law in order to be able to fulfill the Law. "Now when the days of her purification according to the law of Moses were completed, they brought Him to Jerusalem to present Him to the Lord [as it is written in the law of the Lord: "Every male that opens the womb shall be called holy to the Lord"], and to offer a sacrifice according to what is said in the law of the Lord, 'A pair of turtledoves or two young pigeons'" (Lk. 2:22 – 24).

It is recorded that on the day that Jesus was dedicated at the Temple in Jerusalem, both Simeon and Anna the prophetess bore witness to the Child Jesus as being the Messiah and Savior of their people.

Jesus, the Early Years:

Following the dedication of Jesus at the Temple in Jerusalem, Joseph and Mary returned to Nazareth of Galilee. "And the Child grew and became strong in spirit, filled with wisdom; and the grace of God was upon Him" (v. 40).

Joseph, the stepfather of Jesus, was a carpenter by trade, and Jesus would follow in the occupation of His stepfather Joseph. This is revealed to us in the gospel of Mark, when Jesus was rejected by His own people, the Nazarenes. "Is this not the carpenter, the Son of Mary, and brother of James, Joses, Judas, and Simon? And are not His sisters here with us?"... So they were offended at Him. But Jesus said to them, "A prophet is not without honor except in his own country, among his own relatives, and in his own house".

Besides learning the trade of his stepfather, Jesus must have also been a devout student of the synagogue in Nazareth. Being the Son of the Most High, with a spirit as pure as the word of God itself, He would have excelled in knowledge far beyond His contemporaries and His rabbinical tutors.

We find an example of this young Boy's already accumulated wisdom in Luke 2:41 – 50. At the age of twelve, Jesus went up to Jerusalem with His family to celebrate the Passover Feast. It is recorded that when the days of the Feast were completed Joseph and Mary gathered the family together and headed back to Nazareth. After a day's travel they looked for Jesus among their relatives and others from their region who had traveled to Judea with them. When they could not find Him among their people, they traveled back to Jerusalem. After three days of searching for their missing Son, they found Him in the temple sitting in the midst of the rabbis, listening to them and asking them questions. "And all who heard Him were astonished at His understanding and answers. So when they saw Him, they were amazed; and His mother said to Him, 'Son, why have You done this to us? Look, Your father and I have sought You anxiously'. And He said to them, 'Why did you seek Me? Did you not know that I must be about My Father's business?'".

Needless to say that this three-day question and answer session with Jesus and the teachers of the temple did not sit very well with Joseph and Mary. When Jesus went back to Nazareth with them, He was subject to their parental rule and watchful eye.

It is recorded that as Jesus grew in stature He also increased in wisdom, and found favor with both God and man (v. 52).

These years spent working His trade and studying in the synagogues would enlighten Him not only in the word, but also in the nature and mindset of those He dwelt with. Galilee was a region that hosted many small towns and fishing villages. He, in the stewardship of His stepfather Joseph of Galilee, Jesus must have met an array of colorful and offbeat characters from the fishermen, to the vendors, to the housewives, and to the elders. Jesus would walk among these Galileans for nearly thirty years before He went on to proclaim the kingdom of God to His spiritual oppressed generation.

John the Baptist:

In the fifteenth year of Tiberius Caesar (about 29 AD), John, the son of Zacharias the priest, went out and began to baptize the children of Abraham in the waters of the Jordan River. In those days, many flocked to John, believing him to be a prophet and deliverer of Israel. From the commoner to the tax collector to the soldier and even those of the rabbinical priesthood. Some went to hear his words to glorify God, others went to spy and bring back reports of John's doings to the high priest and the Sanhedrin (council of religious elders) of his doings.

After a time, the council sent priests from Jerusalem to ask John who he was. When they asked him "He confessed, and did not deny, but confessed, "I am not the Christ". And they asked him, "What then? Are you Elijah?" He said, "I am not". "Are you the Prophet?" and he answered, "No". Then they said to him, "Who you are, that we may give an answer to those who sent us? What do you say about yourself?" He said:

"I am 'The voice of one crying in the wilderness: "Make strait the way of the Lord"' As the prophet Isaiah said" (Jn. 1:20 – 23)

John, by quoting this particular scripture in Isaiah, revealed to the Pharisees and those whom he was baptizing along the Jordan that he was not the Light, but was sent to bear witness to the Light that would be sent upon his people Israel. As they, the Pharisees, continued to contend with John as to where his authority came from, he said this: "...I indeed baptize you with water; but One mightier than I is coming, whose sandal strap I am not worthy to loose. He will baptize you with the Holy Spirit and fire." (Lk. 3:16).

The high priest and Sanhedrin's concern with John was short-lived. Not long after John baptized Jesus, Herod the tetrarch had John arrested for condemning his relationship with Herodias, his brother Philip's wife (Mk. 6:14 – 29).

Jesus Baptized:

All the people, including Jesus, were eventually baptized. While Jesus prayed, the heavens opened and the Holy Spirit descended in bodily form like a dove upon Him. A voice came from Heaven and said, "You are My beloved Son; in You I am well pleased" (vs. 21 – 22).

Being filled with the Spirit of God, Jesus was led into the wilderness to be tested by the Devil (Satan). He went forty days and forty nights without food, being tested while in a state of physical weakness and mental fatigue (Lk. 4:1 – 13). The most common question asked about Jesus' encounter with Satan is, "Why did God allow Jesus to be tested?" From the time of the Garden of Eden, when Lucifer tempted Adam, to the time of Jesus' encounter with this same Serpent of Old, millions upon millions had fallen at the feet of this indelible creature. His cunning and masterful skills of deception have caused even those of high moral ground to fall to rebellion and self-satisfaction. He was and still is the manipulator of the nations and the conscience of the proud. By him chaos reigns, and by him the righteous are made to fall. Jesus, even though he was the Son of the Most High, was made ready by the Holy Spirit to face His ultimate battle: Himself. In our Lord's weakened state, Satan tested Him in three specific areas: will power, ego and self-pride, and obedience. Jesus passed these three tests with nothing more than His love for His Father, and His perseverance of His kingdom. "Now when the devil had ended every temptation, he departed from Him until an opportune time" (v. 13).

Indeed, Satan is an opportunist. Unfortunately for him, however, another opportunity never presented itself. Not even on that dreadful night of His arrest in the garden of Gethsemane did our Lord falter from His mission. Amen.

Jesus Begins His Ministry:

Jesus, being filled with the Holy Spirit, returned to Galilee and entered Nazareth. As was His custom, Jesus entered the synagogue on the Sabbath and stood up and began to read a passage from the book of Isaiah:

"The Spirit of the Lord is upon Me,
Because He has anointed Me
To preach the gospel to the poor;
He has sent Me to heal the brokenhearted,
To proclaim liberty to the captives
And recovery of sight to the blind,
To set at liberty those who are oppressed;
To proclaim the acceptable year of the Lord"
(Lk. 4:18 – 19).

Once Jesus was finished reading the passage, He closed the book and sat. He then said to them, "Today this Scripture is fulfilled in your hearing". Knowing Jesus to be the Son of Joseph the carpenter, they were bewildered by His words, saying, "Is this not Joseph's Son?" Jesus, seeing the disbelief of His people, the Nazarenes, said this: "Assuredly, I say to you, no prophet is accepted in his own country". Following this statement, the people began to get aroused and they rose up and took Him out of the city to try to destroy Him. However, He passed right through the midst of them and went His way.

Needless to say, He was unable to do any great works among His own people. So, He traveled to Capernaum and began teaching in the synagogues and casting out unclean spirits. It was in Bethsaida, the home of Simon (who He would come to name Peter), Simon's brother Andrew, and the sons of Zebedee, John, and James where Jesus would first begin to gather His disciples. It is recorded in the gospel of John that it was Andrew (a disciple of John the Baptist) who became one of Jesus' first followers. As Jesus traveled through the regions of Galilee, many more disciples joined Him.

"Now it came to pass in those days that He went out to a mountain to pray, and continued all night in prayer to God. And when it was day, He called His disciples to Himself; and from them He chosen twelve whom He also named apostles". These twelve were named: Simon Peter, Andrew, John, James, Philip, Bartholomew, Matthew, Thomas, James (the son of Alphaeus), Simon the Zealot, Judas (the son of James), and Judas Iscariot. These were the twelve chosen out of His many disciples and followers who were to bring His teachings to the four corners of the earth. We as believers are all Disciples of Christ. The simple meaning of the word "disciple" is student: one who studies. The word or title "apostle" given to these twelve who were exalted by Jesus over His other disciples can have several different meanings. However, the most important one, I believe, was to continue teaching His disciples of their day and organizing His church. It is recorded in Acts that on the Day of Pentecost that followed Christ's crucifixion, the disciples numbered about one hundred twenty.

Jesus' ministry is believed to have lasted about three to three and a half years. During that time, Jesus raised the dead, caused the lame to walk, the blind to see, the deaf to hear, and the mute to speak. He cast out demons and trampled over snakes and serpents. He was successful in spreading the good news (gospel) through Judaea, Samaria, Galilee, and beyond the Jordan River. But what was Jesus' true mission? Yes, He set the captive free and became a Champion to the oppressed, but what was His true goal and purpose to the cross? The true goal and purpose for our Lord's ministry was and is still to find those who will reign with Him on the Seventh Day, the Millennial Sabbath. (The fourteenth day of our Lord's millennial calendar).

Jesus was recorded as saying this in Mark 2:27 – 28: "And He said to them, 'The Sabbath was made for man, and not man for the Sabbath.' Therefore the Son of Man is also LORD OF THE SABBATH".

What does this mean, that Jesus is also the Lord of the Sabbath? Jesus came to redeem the seventh day that His brother, Adam, lost to Lucifer when he transgressed upon God's law and ate from the tree that was forbidden to him. The Lord God sanctified the seventh day and rested upon it. As God rested, the heavenly and earthly realms fell to corruption under the hand of Lucifer, who is now called Satan. Man, in a state of corruption since this fall, was not deemed worthy to enter into the seventh day of the second millennium until Jesus found victory on the cross at Calvary (Golgotha). There Christ defeated sin and, being raised on the third day, defeated both Death and Hades. By our Lord's victory at Calvary, and He being the final atonement, the redemption of man was at hand. He, our Savior, was made worthy to rule on the seventh day as King of kings and Lord of Lords.

The following was recorded in Psalms 95, concerning the rejection of Israel's rebellious children. "Do not harden your hearts as in the day of rebellion, as in the day of trial in the wilderness, when your fathers tested Me; they tried Me, though they saw [M]y work. For forty years I was grieved with that generation. And said, 'It is a people who go astray in their hearts, and they do not know My ways.' So I swore in My wrath, 'They shall not enter My rest'"

(vv. 8 – 11).

Then who is able to enter His rest? Those who have been given—or are yet to be given—to Jesus, to reign with Him on the seventh day are able to enter His rest.

Who is Worthy:

Following the Lord's crucifixion, when He was nailed to the cross at Calvary and placed between two criminals (Dimas on His right and Gestas on His left). This was about the third hour of the day (9:00am) and, by being so badly beaten by the Roman soldiers, His strength gave out about the ninth hour of the day (3:00pm). It was in this ninth hour that He gave up His Spirit to God.

"And when Jesus had cried out with a loud voice, He said, 'Father, into Your hands I commit My spirit'. Having said this, He breath His last" (Lk. 23:46). After breathing His last breath and giving up His spirit, Joseph of Arimathea (a council member) went to Pilate, the governor of Judaea and asked for the body of Jesus...Joseph wrapped the body of Jesus in a linen cloth and placed Him in a tomb near Calvary. On the third day, Jesus rose and was seen several times by His disciples. After forty days had passed since His resurrection, Jesus was taken up in a cloud and ascended into Heaven. Before He ascended, however, He commissioned them to tarry in Jerusalem until the Promise of the Holy Spirit came upon them.

"Then He said to them, 'Go into all the world and preach the gospel to every creature.' He who believes and is baptized will be saved; but he who does not believe will be condemned...And these signs will follow those who believe: In My name they will cast out demons; they will speak with new tongues; they will take up serpents; and if they drink anything deadly, it will by no means hurt them; they will lay hands on the sick, and they will recover'" (Mk. 16:15 – 18).

The baptism spoken of by Jesus was not the baptism of water as John baptized in the Jordan. The Lord was speaking of the baptism of the Word, the spoken word that falls upon the hearing of men. It is as a seed that takes root in the hearts of men to produce a crop of righteousness in Christ Jesus. If this seed (word) falls on good ground (hearts), it acts as a two-edged sword dividing in two the soul and the spirit. This is the baptism of the Word. This baptism comes upon those who accept the word of God with an open and receptive heart. They are those who will reign with Christ Jesus on the seventh day (See the parable of the sower, Lk. 8:4 – 8, 11 - 15).

It is written that, "For many are called, but few are chosen". Not all who claim to be Christians and devout followers of Christ will be saved, but only those who the Lord has chosen to reign with His Son on the Sabbath Day. Many will fall by the wayside on that great and awesome Day of the Lord. Jesus prophesied this of the Day: "Not everyone who says to Me, 'Lord, Lord', shall enter into the kingdom of heaven, but he who does the will of My Father in heaven. 'Many will say to Me in that day, 'Lord, Lord have we not prophesied in Your name, cast out demons in Your name, and done many wonders in Your name?'...'And then I will declare to them, 'I never knew you; depart from Me, you who practice lawlessness!'" (Mt. 7:21 – 23).

Jesus also prayed this the night He was betrayed by Judas Iscariot in the garden of Gethsemane: "I have manifested Your name to the men whom You have given to Me out of the world. They were Yours, You gave them to Me, and they have kept Your Word. Now they have known that all things which You gave Me are from You. For I have given to them the words which You have given to Me; and they have received them, and have known surely that I come forth from You; and they have believed that You sent Me. **"I pray for them. I do not pray for the world but for those whom You have given to Me, for they are Yours"** (Jn. 17:6 – 9).

Who are these that were given to Jesus from the world? Our Lord said this concerning those who have been given to Him by His Father: "You will know them by their fruits". He who comes forth bearing fruits of righteousness, such as love, joy, peace, long-suffering, kindness, goodness, faithfulness, gentleness, and self-control. These are those who have been crucified in the flesh by Christ Jesus, with its passions and desires. They have been made worthy to walk with Christ for a thousand years. And if you yourself bear these fruits of righteousness in the name of Christ Jesus, stay diligent in your walk, and ready yourself to enter His rest.

"Today, if you hear His voice:
Do not harden your hearts as in the rebellion."

Let us therefore be diligent to enter that rest, lest anyone fall according to the same example of disobedience."

(Ps 95:7-8; Heb 4:11)

Chapter 14

The Reign of the Twelve Apostles:

Our Lord ascended into heaven from Mount Olivet, in the presence of His disciples. As soon as the Lord was taken from their sight, they returned to Jerusalem, as instructed by the Lord. They were to wait for the Promise before leaving Jerusalem. "And when they had entered, they went up into the upper room where they were staying: Peter, James, John, and Andrew; Phillip and Thomas; Bartholomew and Matthew; James the son of Alphaeus and Simon the Zealot; and Judas the son of James" (Acts 1:13). Also in their company were the women, Mary (the Lord's mother), and His brothers. Everyone prayed and continued in supplication, waiting for the Promise of the Holy Spirit to come upon them as Jesus had instructed. Altogether the disciples numbered about one hundred twenty men and women. Of the chosen twelve apostles, however, only eleven remained.

Judas Iscariot, who betrayed the Lord for thirty pieces of silver, had hung himself from a tree. After Judas returned the money he had taken from the high priest in Jerusalem to betray Jesus, he went and hung himself from a tree. It is recorded in Acts 1:18 that he fell headlong and burst open in the middle so that all of his entrails gushed out. This is what Jesus had said about the one who would betray Him: "...but woe to that man by whom the Son of Man is betrayed! It would have been good for that man if he had never been born" (Mk. 14:21).

The Twelve Chosen:

Knowing the office of Judas Iscariot must be filled, Peter stood up in the midst of the one hundred twenty disciples and picked two disciples from the hundred and twenty who had been with Jesus from the very beginning. The names of the two men chosen were Justus and Matthias. So they stood in prayer to the Lord, and cast lots. The lots fell upon Matthias, and he became one of the twelve apostles, taking the place of Judas Iscariot.

The Day of Pentecost:

After tarrying in Jerusalem for ten days as per instructions of the Lord, Pentecost was upon them. The one hundred twenty prayed in one accord as they were gathered together. Pentecost fell on the Sunday following 7 Sabbaths from the resurrection of Christ Jesus. It is the feast of the first fruits of the wheat harvest. This same feast day of the year 32 or 33 AD would become the birth of our modern-day church. The apostles were to become the first fruits of the ministry of the Holy Spirit.

It is recorded in Acts 2:1 – 4 that as they prayed in one accord, the Spirit of God fell upon them. "And suddenly there came a sound from heaven, as a rushing mighty wind, and it filled the whole house where they were sitting. Then there appeared to them divided tongues, as of fire, and one say upon each of them. And they were all filled with the Holy Spirit and began to speak with other tongues, as the Spirit gave them utterance." All one hundred twenty disciples were now baptized in the Holy Spirit. From then on, speaking in other tongues of both men and angels would be the sign of this baptism to all future generations.

It is recorded that on that day Peter rose up to testify to the multitudes and many came to the Lord. Men were cut to the heart and the baptism of the Spirit was upon them. "And that day about three thousand souls were added to them" (Acts 2:41). The Power of the Most High was now upon them and the Disciples of Christ Jesus were made ready to begin their ministries that would carry to the ends of the earth.

The Spirit rested heavily on the shoulders of Peter. He healed the sick, cast out the demonic, and raised the dead. It was not long, however, before the Sanhedrin took notice of his activities and had him arrested for preaching Jesus to the multitudes. "Now when they saw the boldness of Peter and John, and perceived that they were uneducated and untrained men, they marveled. And they realized that they had been with Jesus" (Acts 4:13). However, having nothing with which to bring accusation against Peter, they let him and John go with a stern warning not to preach the name of Jesus any longer. This would not be the last time Peter was arrested. Many trials and tribulations were about to fall upon not only Peter but the entire following of the sect of the Nazarene.

In the beginning days of the fledgling church, a great persecution arose in the church led by a young Pharisee named Saul. Saul first consented to the stoning of Stephen, a devout follower of Christ Jesus, and then began a vicious assault against the church. Saul caused so much havoc on the fledgling church that he caused the followers of Jesus to scatter throughout all the surrounding regions of Judaea to escape his arrest. Knowing that some of the followers of Jesus fled as far as Damascus, Saul went to the high priest to write letters to the synagogues of Damascus so that he may arrest any follower that he found of Jesus, and bring them back to Jerusalem.

As Saul neared Damascus to arrest those of the "Way", he was stuck down on the road: "...and suddenly a light shone around him from heaven. Then he fell to the ground and heard a voice saying to him, 'Saul, Saul, why are you persecuting Me?' And he said 'Who are You, Lord?' Then the Lord said 'I am Jesus, whom you are persecuting. It is hard for you to kick against the goads' So he, trembling and astonished, said, 'Lord what You want me to do?' Then the Lord said to him, 'Arise and go into the city, and you will be told what you must do'" (Acts 9:3 – 6).

Saul immediately rose to his feet and, being led by his companions, went in to the city to wait on the Lord's word. At this time, Saul was temporarily blind from the shining light that illuminated Christ Jesus on the Damascus road. Saul was three days in Damascus in prayer and fasting. On the third day the Lord went to His disciple Ananias, in a vision, who was there in Damascus, to go to Saul and lay hands on him. Ananias was first leery concerning Saul, knowing the havoc he brought down upon the church, but the Lord reassured him that Saul was a chosen vessel to bear His name to the Gentiles.

"And Ananias went his way and entered the house; and laying his hands on him he said, 'Brother Saul, the Lord Jesus, who appeared to you on the road as you came, has sent me that you may receive your sight and be filled with the Holy Spirit.' Immediately there fell from his eyes something like scales, and he received his sight at once; and he arose and was baptized" (vv. 17 – 18).

Some ask why the Lord would choose such a man that persecuted His children, even to death, to bring His word to the Gentiles and bestow upon him eternal life. To answer this question, we must first look upon Saul's mission of destruction from his point of view. Saul, being a Pharisee and a devout man of God, believed that those who followed the Way (the sect of the Nazarene) were nothing more than heretics who were perverting his religion and beliefs of his fathers before him. Saul did not know of the teaching of Jesus, nor was he about to let these followers of His blasphemy against his beloved Rabbinical Order. Saul believed himself to be a champion of God, not a persecutor of His Son. Jesus knew that Saul's persecution of His saints was being committed out of Saul's ignorance of His word. Jesus just had to knock him down and let him see the light so He could win his heart. Saul's one great attribute, that I believe Jesus needed to harness for His own purpose, was Saul's persistence. Our Lord knew that once the truth was revealed to him, that he would never relent in regards to spreading His word to every corner of the known world. Saul would indeed become a champion of Christ. "'...for he is a chosen vessel of Mine to bear My name before Gentiles, kings, and the children of Israel. "For I will show him how many things he must suffer for My name's sake'" (vv. 15 – 16).

As Saul's conversion was about to turn the hearts of his own people against him, Peter was being made ready to bring the Word to the Gentiles.

The Beast:

Although we are not certain of the year that Saul (who was also know n as Paul) was converted to Christianity, I believe it was some time at the end of Tiberus' reign in 37 AD. Paul's ministry spanned the course of four emperors of Rome, Tiberus being the second of these (the second noble horn of Daniel's goat and the second head of the beast of Revelation). He reigned from the years 14 AD to 37 AD. The third noble horn and the third head of the beast was Caligula, who reigned from 37 AD to 41 AD. The fourth and last noble horn of the goat and the fourth head of the beast was Claudius Caesar, who reigned from 41 AD to 54 AD.

It is recorded in Acts 24 that when Paul was arrested in Jerusalem during the latter years of his ministry (for being accused of sedition by his Roman captive) he appealed his case to Caesar when brought before Festus, the governor of Judaea. Paul also appealed his case to Caesar when he was brought before King Agrippa and his wife Bernice. Unfortunately, the name of the emperor that Paul was appealing to was not properly recorded in the scriptures:

"But when Paul appealed to be reserved for the decision of Augustus, I commanded him to be kept till I could send him to Caesar" (v. 21).

Augustus Caesar reigned from 27 BC to 14 BC, so he could not have been the Caesar of Paul's time. However, Augustus' great nephew Nero may have been emperor in the last years of Paul's ministry. Nero became emperor of Rome in the year 54 AD, following the death of his stepfather Claudius (who was believed to have been poisoned by Nero's mother in order for Nero to become emperor). Nero is the little horn recorded in Daniel 8 who comes out of one of the four noble horns. Being the great nephew of Augustus, he came forth from Augustus, not his stepfather Claudius.

Below is a speculative image of the beast in the later years of Paul's more than twenty-year ministry.

Chapter 15

The Gentiles Receive the Holy Spirit:

It is recorded in Acts 9:36 – 43 that Peter was asked to go to Joppa to help a certain disciple named Tabitha who fell ill and died. When peter reached Joppa, he went up into the upper room where they had the body of Tabitha laid out. Peter asked everyone who were mourning over her body to leave the room. Then Peter got down on his knees and began to pray. "And turning to the body he said, 'Tabitha, arise.' And she opened her eyes, and when she saw Peter she sat up. Then he gave her his hand and lifted her up; and when he had called the saints and the widows, he presented her alive" (vv. 40 – 41).

Peter stayed in Joppa for a time at the house of Simon the tanner. At that time, there was a Roman centurion named Cornelius living in Caesarea. He was a devout man of God giving generously in his community, helping his neighbors, and in constant prayer and supplication to God. One afternoon, at about the ninth hour (3:00pm), Cornelius was in prayer when he received a vision of an angel coming in and saying to him, "Cornelius!" "And when he observed him, he was afraid, and said, 'What is it lord?' So he said to him, 'Your prayers and your alms have come up to a memorial before God...Now send men to Joppa, and send for Simon whose surname is Peter...He is lodging with Simon, a tanner, whose house is by the sea. He will tell you what you must do'" (Acts 10:4 – 6). Once the angel departed from him he went and told two of his servants and one of his soldiers what had happened and then sent them on their way to Joppa to fetch Peter.

The following day, Peter was up on the rooftop of Simon's house in prayer, at about the sixth hour (12:00pm), and a vision came to him. He saw what looked like a great sheet coming down from heaven, bound on its four corners. "In it were all kinds of four-footed animals of the earth, wild beast, creeping things, and birds of the air. And a voice came to him, 'Rise, Peter; kill and eat'" (Acts 10:12 – 13).

Peter answered and said, "Not so", for Peter had never eaten anything unclean. Three times Peter saw this sheet descend and ascend into the heavens. The voice spoke to him again, saying, "What God has cleansed you must not call common". Through this vision of the unclean creatures the Lord was readying Peter to go to the Gentiles. This is because until this vision was revealed to Peter, it was unlawful for a Jew to eat unclean food or even go to an unclean person (Gentile).

Immediately following Peter's vision, Cornelius' servants reached Simon's house and asked for Peter. They explained to Peter their master's vision and the next day Peter and some of the brethren traveled to Caesarea. As Cornelius awaited their arrival, he gathered together his friends and family members to hear the words of Peter. When Peter arrived with his companions, he began to speak, and as he spoke, the Spirit of God descended on the household of Cornelius. "And those of the circumcision who believed were astonished, as many as came with Peter, because the gift of the Holy Spirit had been poured out on the Gentiles also. For they heard them speaking in tongues magnify God" (vv. 45 – 46).

When Peter arrived back in Jerusalem, he shared what the Lord had done by giving the gift of the Holy Spirit to the Gentiles. "And they glorified God, saying, "Then God has also granted to the Gentiles repentance to life" (11:18).

Following Peter's arrest that is recorded in Acts 12, Peter is no longer mentioned. The reason for Peter's absence in the remaining chapters of Acts is the fact that Luke, the author of Acts, began traveling with Paul. Beginning in chapter 13, Luke shares with us an in-depth journal of Paul's ministry: beginning from his conversion in Damascus to his arrest in Jerusalem and imprisonment in Rome. Most theologians and historians believe Paul was imprisoned in Rome in approximately the year 63 AD. Our Lord prophesied in Acts 9:16: "For I will show him how many things he must suffer for My name's sake." And truly Paul did suffer in and for the namesake of Christ Jesus.

Paul himself recorded his suffering in 2 Corinthians 11: "Are they ministries of Christ?—I speak as a fool—I am more: in labors more abundant, in stripes above measure, in prisons more frequently, in deaths often. From the Jews five times I received forty stripes minus one. Three times I was beaten with rods; once I was stoned; three times I was shipwrecked; a night and a day I have been in the deep; in journeys often, in perils of water, in perils of robbers, in perils of my own countrymen, in perils of the Gentiles, in perils in the city, in perils in the wilderness, in perils in the sea, in perils among false brethren; in weariness and toil, in sleeplessness often, in hunger and in thirst, in fastings often, in cold and nakedness" (vs. 23 – 27). Yes, Paul suffered many things in the name of Christ Jesus, and in the later years of his journey he is again in prison waiting coming judgment from Nero (who was now emperor of Rome).

No historical record confirming Paul's death or continuation of his ministry beyond Luke's account of Paul's two-year house arrest in Rome exists (Acts 28:17 – 31). He may have been released by Nero and continued his ministry to the Romans, or Nero may have kept Paul as a prisoner until his death. In one of his fourteen epistles, Paul mentions his chains: "...inasmuch as both in my chains and in the defense and confirmation of the gospel, you are all partakers with me in grace" (Phil. 1:7).

The Destruction of the Temple:

Paul fought the good fight of faith and may have been one of the last of the apostles of Peter's era to be living during the time of the Jewish Roman War, which occurred between the years 66 AD and 70 AD).

Jesus had prophesied this coming destruction of Jerusalem and the temple during His Olivet discourse of the end of days. "Then Jesus went out and departed from the temple, and His disciples came up to show Him the buildings of the temple/ And Jesus said to them, "Do you not see all these things? Assuredly, I say to you, not one stone shall be left here upon another, that shall not be thrown down" (Mt. 24:1 – 2).

When Jesus and his disciples reached the Mount of Olives, Peter, James, John, and Andrew came to Him in privacy and asked when this thing (the destruction of the temple) would take place. They also wanted to know when the end of time would come, when all things would be completed. Our Lord's discourse begins in Matthew 24:4 – 14, in which he gives the apostles an overall view of the tribulations His followers must endure through the millenniums, until the gospel of the kingdom is preached throughout the entire world; as a witness to all the nations. Only then, when all these things are accomplished, will the end come.

Chapters 15 – 28 of Matthew's gospel, pertain to the great tribulation that was to come upon the Jewish people by their Roman oppressors. This was the destruction of both the temple and the city of Jerusalem in 70 AD. "Therefore when you see the 'abomination of desolation', spoken of by Daniel the prophet, standing in the holy place [the temple]...Then let those in Judea flee to the mountains".

In the year 66 AD, the Jewish people rose up in rebellion against the Romans when Nero placed a statue of himself in the temple. Just as in the days of Judas Maccabeus, when the Hellenist set up an altar to Zeus in the temple, the people revolted. Nero exalted himself as a deity and brought an end to the daily sacrifices that the priest of the temple made to the Lord of Host. As prophesied in Daniel 8:9 – 14, an army was sent by Nero to besiege the city and bring the Jewish people back under submission to Rome.

The destruction of Jerusalem and the tribulation of their people would be so great that Jesus wept over their impending doom. "Now as He drew near, He saw the city and wept over it, saying, 'If I had known, even you, especially in this your day, the things that make for your peace! But now they are hidden from your eyes...For days will come upon you when your enemies will build an embankment around you, surround you and close you in on every side, and level you, and your children within you, to the ground; and they will not leave in you on stone upon another, because you did not know the time of your visitation'" (Lk. 19:41 – 44).

In the year 66 AD, Nero appointed Vespasian to lead the Roman army against the rebellious Jews. Vespasian was given three legions to besiege all of Judaea and the city of Jerusalem. As the revolt continued on, Nero, in the year 68 AD, committed suicide, causing a civil war that brought three emperors to the throne by the following year. However, in the year 69 AD, both the legions of Egypt and Judaea saluted Vespasian as emperor of Rome. The Senate quickly followed. Vespasian was officially made Emperor before the year ended.

Vespasian handed the reins to his son Titus to finish the besieging of Jerusalem and dispersion of the Jewish people throughout the Roman Empire. For about forty-two months, as predicted by Daniel, Jerusalem was encircled by siege walls to prevent any from going out or coming in to the city. The resistance that held the city for the forty-two months behind its fortified walls, fell to all sorts of barbaric behaviors not to starve to death. Our Lord warned the women of those days when all this was to take place: "but woe to those who are pregnant and to those who are nursing babies in those days! For there will be great distress in the land and wrath upon this people" (Mk. 21:23). He said to those that are in Judaea on that day to flee to the mountains and not even to go back down to their house to take any property. He said to those in the fields not to go to their homes for clothing, but to flee and not turn back.

For the hunger struck so bad that those inside the walls of the city began to eat the children to fight off their starvation. They literally pulled the nursing children from the breast of their mothers. The world had never before witnessed the tribulations that fell upon the Jewish people for those forty-two months. When the prophesied forty-two months had ended in the year 70 AD, Titus, who had become his father Vespasian's successor to the throne, broke through the walls of the city, leveled the temple by fire until not one stone was left upon another, as Jesus prophesied. The city of Jerusalem was left in rubble, and those of the city who survived the Roman onslaught were dispersed through the territories of the Roman Empire with their fellow Judeans.

The total dispersion of the Jewish people was completed in approximately the year 73 AD, as ordered by Emperor Vespasian. For nearly two thousand years, the Jews strived through wars and persecutions, such as racism and genocide at the hands of fascist governments and dictators like Hitler and Stalin. Despite the conquest of these genocidal driven dictators, the Israelis began to repopulate the Promised Land. By the year 1947, Israel (formerly Palestine) became an independent state, and by 1967 Jerusalem was its capital city. This return of Israel to Judaea was prophesied by Ezekiel. "Thus says the Lord God: 'Surely I will take the children of Israel from among the nations, wherever they have gone, and will gather them from every side and bring them into their own land; and I will make them one nation in one land'" (37:21 – 22).

The prophecies of Israel are now being brought to fruition in our lifetime. As I also believe, the contents and prophecies of the Book of Revelation will also come to fruition in the first generations of our new millennium. It is the writings of John of Patmos which are the most intriguing to me. John's writings are the culmination of the history of the human race and the entire prophetic allegory of the Biblical record. John wrote this book of consummation during the reign of Vespasian, the sixth head of the beast.

Vespasian reigned from the years 69 AD to 79 AD. It was sometime during his reign that John, who is also called "John the Revelator", was exiled to the Island of Patmos. Here he penned, in rustic Greek prose, one of the greatest prophetic writings of the Bible. This controversial piece of literature has been a topic of debate among historians and theologians throughout the ages. Many scholarly agents of the Bible have renounced the writings of this text as simply metaphoric. I myself, in addition to many of my contemporaries, believe the writing of this text to be an accurate given account of the end of days.

Chapter 16

The Book Revelation:

While exiled on the island of Patmos, John received a series of visions and revelations regarding the end time prophecies of Christ Jesus, His church, and the events leading to His millennial reign. The text, being purposely veiled in both its prophetic visions and almost unattainable timelines, is written in chronological order. It first reveals the state of the seven churches of Asia-minor (present-day Turkey) in the first century AD (Chapters 1 – 3). It then unfolds the seven-year tribulation period in Chapters 4 through 19. In chapter 20:1 – 6, the millennial reign of Christ Jesus is discussed. Finally, the conclusion of Creation when the Lord has completed all His work is unveiled (20:7 – 15, 21 – 22).

The Seven Churches:

"I, John, both your brother and companion in the tribulation and kingdom and patience of Jesus Christ, was on the island that is called Patmos for the word of God and for the testimony of Jesus Christ. I was in the Spirit on the Lord's Day [Sabbath], and I heard behind me a loud voice, as a trumpet, saying, 'I am the Alpha and Omega, the First and the Last', and, 'What you see, write in the book and send it to the seven churches which are in Asia: To Ephesus, to Smyrna, to Pergamos, to Thyatira, to Sardis, to Philadelphia, and to Laodicea'" (1:9 – 11). As soon as John heard this voice he turned to see a glorious Man who identified Himself as the Lord, by saying, "I am the First and the Last...I have the keys of Hades and of Death..." (vs. 17 – 18). Again, the Lord urges John to write what he has seen and the things that are to come.

Why were John's writings to be directed to these seven churches of Asia-Minor? Why not the churches of Judaea or Rome? Why not those of Greece? The most obvious reasoning can be simply the state and condition of these churches after only one generation following Christ's crucifixion. These seven churches have had seven identifying labels or titles added to them over the centuries.

The first church, at Ephesus, has come to be known as "The Loveless Church" because the Lord spoke to John, saying this of the Ephesus church: "...you have left your first love" (2:1 – 7). The second church, at Smyrna, is called "The Persecuted Church" because the Lord had prophesied this concerning the church: "...the devil is about to throw some of you into prison, that you may be tested" (vv. 8 – 11).

The church at Pergamos is known as "The Compromising Church" due to the Lord's words: "But I have a few things against you, because you have there those who hold the doctrine of Balaam" (vv. 12 – 17). The fourth church, at Thyatira, is called "The Corrupt Church" because of the acceptance of sexually immoral behavior among their clergy and parishioners. "Nevertheless I have a few things against you, because you allow that woman Jezebel, who calls herself a prophetess, to teach and seduce My servants to commit sexual immorality" (vv. 18 – 29). The church at Sardis has come to be known as "The Dead Church" because the Lord said: "Be watchful, and strengthen the things which remain, that are ready to die..." (3:1 – 6).

The sixth church, at Philadelphia, is called "The Faithful Church". This is the church that shall ascend into the clouds to meet Christ in the air on the great and awesome Day of the

Lord. Jesus said this about the Philadelphia church: "I know your works. See, I have set before you an open door, and no one can shut it; for you have a little strength, have kept My word, and have not denied My name...Indeed I will make those of the synagogue of Satan, who say they are Jews and are not, but lie—indeed I will make them come and worship before your feet, and to know that I have loved you...Because you have kept My command to preserve, I also will keep you from the hour of trial which shall come upon the whole world, to test those who dwell on the earth" (vv. 7 – 13).

It is the faithful in Christ who will be raptured from the earth to escape the forty-two months of testing that will fall upon the remaining six churches. Do not misinterpret the meaning of the word *church* in regards to these seven churches of Asia-Minor. The scriptures are not referring to a building or particular institution or denomination. They are referring to the people who are from every corner of the earth who have been chosen to reign with Christ Jesus.

For example, the seventh and last church the scriptures speak about is the church at Laodicea. This seventh church has come to be known as "The Lukewarm Church". Jesus said this of the church: "....you are neither cold nor hot..." (vv. 14 – 22). Do you believe those who are lukewarm will be chosen to reign with Christ Jesus? There will be people from each church who will be worthy to walk with Christ through His millennial reign. Jesus spoke this in chapter 3:4 to the dead church: "You have a few names even in Sardis who have not defiled their garments; and they shall walk with Me in white, for they are worthy".

Who are those people that Jesus is speaking of? Jesus' followers who have been cut to the heart by the word of God and are filled with the anointing power of the Holy Spirit will walk with Christ. These are the people who will be found faithful and true at the coming of our Lord Jesus. They will be taken up from every church, religious institution, and denomination. No one worthy will be left behind, and those people of the remaining churches who are left behind will be tested by the tribulations that are to fall upon the entire earth. Those people who have walked through the tribulation period and have been found worthy will be taken at the end with those of the resurrection.

These warnings that have been given to the seven churches of Asia-Minor in the days of John the Revelator are the same warnings that are intended for the seven churches in the days preceding the seven-year tribulation period. These writings to the seven churches are what we consider to be dual prophesies. These once-seven churches that were found in these seven cities of antiquity are now spread through the seven continents of the earth. From the Arctic to the Antarctic, churches have been erected under the beliefs of denomination churches and institutions that have failed drastically in their attempts to save souls. Unfortunately, these same characteristics that plagued the remaining six churches of Asia-Minor now plague the churches of the seven continents.

When the time of the end is coming upon you (you who are faithful), take heed of the warnings to these seven churches and be careful not to fall to their hypocrisies.

Chapter 17

The Seven-Year Tribulation Period:

The prophetic timeline of the tribulation period, with its days and months, cannot be properly determined using our modern-day calendar. In both Daniel's time and (most likely) John's time, days, months, and years were kept by the Jewish Lunar calendar. This consisted of twelve thirty-day months, totaling a 360-day year. This means that the tribulation period would consist of 84 thirty-day months, bringing the total number of days to 2,520. It is recorded in Revelation 12:6 that the women (Israel) fled into the wilderness for 1,260 days. This would be half of the time of the tribulation period, forty-two months of the lunar calendar. Using the lunar calendar, we can form an accurate formula of prophetic dates surrounding the major events of John's prophecies. This means that the scholars and theologians of the end times must put away their modern-day calendars and implement the use of the lunar calendar of Daniel's day. The question is, when will be the time to implement this prophetic calendar? An attempt to answer this will be made in the ending discourse. For now, however, this chapter will continue by opening the seven-year tribulation period with the Lamb of God taking the scroll from the Lord's hand.

The Throne Room:

Following the warnings given to the seven churches, John is taken up into the throne room of Heaven. "Immediately I was in the Spirit; and behold, a throne set in heaven, and One sat on the throne. And He who sat there was like a jasper and a sardius stone in appearance; and there was a (rainbow around the throne, in appearance like an emerald. Around the thrones were twenty-four thrones, and on the throne I saw twenty-four elders sitting, clothed in white robes; and they had crowns of gold on their heads" (4:2 – 4).

John writes that he sees a rainbow around the throne. This rainbow is the sign of the covenant that the Lord God made with Noah and his descendants—that he would never again destroy the earth by water (Gen. 9:13 – 14). John also records seeing an additional twenty-four thrones and twenty-four elders sitting upon them. These are the twelve patriarchs of Israel and the twelve apostles of Christ Jesus. Jesus said this to His apostles concerning these thrones: "Assuredly I saw to you, that in the regeneration, when the Son of Man sits on the throne of His glory, you who have followed Me will also sit on twelve thrones, judging the twelve tribes of Israel" (Mt. 19:28). It is also recorded in Revelation 21:12 – 15 that on the twelve gates of the New Jerusalem will be written the twelve names of the patriarchs of Israel and, on its twelve foundations, the twelve apostles of Christ Jesus. John also records seeing four living creatures that surround the thrones saying day and night:

"Holy, holy, holy,

Lord God Almighty,

Who was and is and is to come!"

Jesus Takes the Scroll:

"And I saw in the right hand of Him who sat on the throne a scroll written inside and on the back, sealed with seven seals...Then He came and took the scroll out of the hand of Him who sat on the throne" (5:1, 8).

Jesus takes the scroll that is sealed with seven seals from the hand of His Father. In the hidden writes of this scroll are the announcements of the seven trumpet blasts and the final seven bowl judgments that must be cast upon the earth. Jesus is worthy to take the scroll and begins to break its seals to release what is to come upon the earth. The first four of the seven seals to be broken are to release the Four Horsemen of the Apocalypse. These Four Horsemen will bring havoc upon the earth for the entire span of the tribulation period. Death and Hades will be the end to all those who follow the Beast, and remain disobedient to the Lord of Host.

"We'll discuss the four horsemen in the next chapter".

Chapter 18

The Reign of the Four Horsemen:

The First Seal:

On the seventeenth day of the seventh month of the first year of the tribulation period, Jesus will break the first of the seven seals. Upon breaking the seal, the first of the Four Horsemen of the Apocalypse will be released upon the earth. "And I looked, and behold, a white horse. He who sat on it had a bow; and a crown was given to him, and he went out conquering and to conquer" (Rev. 6:2). For 2,520 days, this spirit of the Conqueror will ride to the four corners of the earth bringing the spirit of war to its kingdoms; and a conquering spirit to its leaders.

The Second Seal:

On the first day of the tenth month of the first year of the tribulation period, Jesus will break the second seal, releasing the Second Horseman. "Another horse, fiery red, went out. And it was granted to the one who sat on it to take peace from the earth, and that the people should kill one another; and there was given to him a great sword" (v. 4). This spirit of conflict will join the first rider to bring additional unrest and confusion to an already unstable earthly political climate.

The Third Seal:

On the first day of the first month of the second year of the tribulation period, Jesus will break the third seal, releasing the Third Horseman. "When He opened the third seal, I heard the third creature say, 'Come and see'. So I looked, and behold, a black horse, and he who sat on it had a pair of scales in his hand. And I heard a voice in the midst of the four living creatures saying, 'A quart of wheat for a denarius, and three quarts of barley for a denarius; and do not harm the oil and the wine'" (vv. 5 – 6).

This rider, who holds the scales in his hand, is a representation of the nations who will hold the starving world populations in control. The nation or nations whose food supply is still not depleted in the beginning years of tribulation will gain control over their starving neighbors. This will cause the poorer and undeveloped nations to be dominated by the stronger and much more adapted agricultural nations. We see this happening now on our world stage—countries such as our own great nation, America. We are sending millions of tons of wheat, corn, and medical aid to most of the impoverished countries of our earth. During the tribulation period, disaster relief will become an everyday occurrence and the scarcity of food and fresh water a reality.

The Fourth Seal:

On the twenty-seventh day of the second month of the second year of the tribulation period, Jesus will break the fourth of the seven seals releasing the last Horseman. "So I looked, and behold, a pale horse. And the name of him who sat on it was Death, And Hades followed with him. And power was given to them over one fourth of the earth, to kill with the sword, with hunger, with death, and the beast of the earth" (v. 8).

This fourth and final rider follows the three who go before him, who bring political unrest, war, and famine to the earth. These four riders of the Apocalypse will be sent out to the four corners of the earth to accelerate these coming plagues on the earth. Blessed is he who makes it to the end of these things. His reward will be in Heaven.

The four dates that I have revealed to you regarding the breaking of the first four seals of the tribulation period were revealed to me by the Spirit. Through revelation after revelation, the Spirit kept bringing me back to Noah and the flood, in Genesis chapters 7 and 8. Understanding that the flood event of Genesis was the first cleansing/baptism of the earth, I began to assimilate some of the dates kept by Noah with the second and final cleansing/baptism of the earth.

The date of the breaking of the first seal, 7/17/00, is recorded in Genesis 8:4. The second date, 10/1/00, is recorded in verse 5. The third date, 1/1/1, is recorded in verse 13, and the final date, 2/27/1, is recorded in verse 14. These four dates revealed to me by the Spirit span a total of 220 days of the Jewish calendar. You may be asking yourself, why are these dates so prevalent to these end-time prophecies? They correlate to Daniel's prophecy of the "Broken Horn" in chapter 8. "...an army was given over to the [little] horn to oppose the daily sacrifices..." How long will the vision be, concerning the daily sacrifices and the transgression of desolation—the giving of both the sanctuary and the host to be trampled underfoot? And he said to me, "For two thousand three hundred days; then the sanctuary shall be cleansed."

In the time of Nero, the sanctuary was the temple in Jerusalem. In the time of the end, however, when the second "Little Horn" will come to reign on the earth, the entire earth will be considered the sanctuary. This is because at the time of the end, the entire earth will be filled with the word of God, with His witnesses.

The seven-year tribulation period spans 2,520 days. If we subtract the 220 days, we are left with the prophesied 2,300 days of Daniel's prophecy of the "Little Horn". On the twenty-seventh day of the second month of the second year of the tribulation period, the reign of the Four Horsemen of the Apocalypse will begin. They will wreak their havoc on every corner of the world, leaving no people, nation, or even tribe unscathed by their plagues of hunger, war, and death. The world will see trials and tribulation never before seen that will be brought by the hands of these four horsemen. Those who keep their faith in Christ Jesus to the end, however, will be preserved and will reign with Him through all eternity. Amen.

Chapter 19

The Rapture:

The word *rapture* is not found away in the contents of scriptures, but has come to be associated with those who will be caught up in the clouds to meet the Lord in the air. Paul writes of this event in his first epistle to the Thessalonians. Although the word *rapture* is associated with this event of the dead, who sleep in Christ Jesus, being resurrected and taken up into the clouds with the living which will occur near the end of the tribulation period, following the last trumpet blast, I associate the word with an event that will take place in the mid-tribulation period. I believe that this will occur on the third day of the third month of the third year of tribulation. The event recorded in Thessalonians is associated with the "Reaping of the Angels", which will occur three days, three months, and three years from the time of the rapture (6/6/06).

Unlike the previous four dates I received concerning the breaking of the first four seals, this date of 3/3/03 cannot be found in the biblical record. It is derived from the culmination of three separate stories of antiquity.

The first revelation I received concerning this date was revealed to me in the book of Genesis, regarding Israel's 430 years in Egypt. Jacob and his children lived thirty years in abundance under the governorship of Joseph before they were met with four hundred years of bondage and servitude (30/400).

The second revelation I received also came to me from the book of Genesis. After crossing the Red Sea, Israel traveled three months through the wilderness before reaching Mt. Sinai. In this three-month period, Israel witnessed many signs and wonders and, when departing from Mt. Sinai, faced forty years of plagues and death caused by their disobedience (3/40).

The third and final revelation came from the book of Jonah. Jonah walked three days through Nineveh preaching repentance, and for forty days the Ninevites repented in sackcloth and ashes and were saved (3/40).

These three separate stories revealed to me two different sets of numbers. The first set is of the 3 threes and the second is of the 3 fours. This brings me to two separate dates, 3/3/03 and 4/4/04. The revelation is this: The beginning three years, three months, and three days of the tribulation will be a time of abundance, signs, and repentance. The remaining four years, four months, and four days of the tribulation period, however, will be a time of bondage, followed by plagues, death, famines, and starvation. However, the first four years, four months and four days of the over-seven-year period will still be a time for repentance. Woe to those who do not repent, for their condemnation will be great.

The Breaking of the Fifth and Sixth Seals:

Fifth Seal:

"When he opened the fifth seal, I saw under the altar the souls of those who had been slain for the word of God and for his testimony which they held. And they cried with a loud voice, saying, 'How long, O Lord, holy and true, until You judge and avenge our blood on those who dwell on the earth?' Then a white robe was given to each of them; and it was said to them that they should rest a little while longer, until both the number of their fellow servants and their brethren, who would be killed as they were, was completed" (vv. 9 -11).

The cry of the martyrs has been heard millions of times over the past two millennia, from the days of the Jewish/Roman persecutions of the Christians to the martyrs of today (from the Philippines to Sudan). Christian persecution will continue until every last child of God is brought up into the clouds to remain in the air with Jesus. However, as Christ acknowledges in verse 11, the time of the martyrs will not be completed until the persecution of the saints is completed. So, the question remains as to who is taken in the mid-tribulation period. It will be those followers of Christ who have been cut to the heart by the word of God and baptized into the ministry of the Holy Spirit. This is the faithful church that Christ spoke of in Revelation 3:10. "Because you have kept My command to persevere, I also will keep you from the hour of trial which shall come upon the whole world, to test those who dwell on the earth."

The Sixth Seal (3/3/03):

On the third day of the third month of the third year of the tribulation period, Jesus will break the sixth seal and the earth shall be raptured. "I looked when He opened the sixth seal, and behold, there was a great earthquake; and the sun became black as sackcloth of hair, and the moon became like blood. And the stars of heaven fell to the earth, as a fig tree drops its late figs when it is shaken by a mighty wind. Then the sky receded as a scroll when it is rolled up, and every mountain and island was moved out of place. And the kings of the earth, and the great men, rich men, the commanders, the mighty men, every slave and every free man, hid themselves in the caves and in the rocks of the mountains, and said to the mountains, 'Fall on us and hide us from the face of Him who sits on the throne and from the wrath of the

Lamb! For the great day of His wrath has come, and who is able to stand?'" (vv. 12 – 17).

What is it that the men of the earth are going to see at the breaking of this sixth seal? We know that there is going to be a great earthquake of such magnitude that the world has never seen before. It will move every island and mountain out of its place. Every man will see the Son of Man coming on His throne. In addition, on this great and awesome Day of the Lord, every eye will see the saints of Christ Jesus taken up into the clouds by mighty whirlwinds. Elijah the prophet was taken up into heaven in the same manner, as recorded in 2 Kings 2:11: "Then it happened, as they continued on and talked, that suddenly a chariot of fire appeared with horses of fire, and separated the two of them [Elijah and Elisha]; and Elijah went up by a whirlwind into heaven".

I have received two conscious-visions of this whirlwind. The two visions I had while I was fully conscience came to me while I was sitting in a park in Western Massachusetts. During the summer months of the year 2000, I was at work on my first manuscript regarding this same subject. Every afternoon I would go to the park and sit on the wooden benches, and often meditating on scriptures pertaining to my studies. One afternoon I was alone, in a quieted form of meditation, when a large funnel appeared about a dozen feet from the bench I was resting on. The mouth of the funnel stood directly in front of me and I felt that I could just get up off the bench and walk into its mouth. The scene was very peaceful and surreal. The circular mouth of the funnel sat on top of the grassy field. Its diameter was about eight feet and its trunk shot almost straight up into the sky. The trunk seemed to twist more into a vertical angle as it united with the clouds.

A few weeks later the same vision reappeared in this same manner as I was again meditating on the park bench. You may think that when you hear of a whirlwind or wind funnel that there would be a certain amount of violence connected to it. However, this was not a typical whirlwind that brings such destruction; this one brings salvation to those who have been chosen to enter it.

How Many Will Be Taken?

Presently dwelling on the earth are about six billion people of which about one-third claim to be Christians. The question raised is how many of the living will be taken at the time of the Rapture and how many of the living, along with the resurrected, will be taken at the time of the reaping of the angels.

During the summer of 2000, one of my students came to me with a dream that he had received the night before. He told me that in the dream, he entered a large church [building] in which he saw myself and another man lighting candles. As he approached us he asked me if he would be taken up with the two percent or six percent. In the dream, I answered him by saying "The two percent".

The dream was clear in its relationship to both the Rapture and the Reaping, but a search of the scriptures would result in its proper interpretation. I immediately calculated 6 billion multiplied by 2 percent. The result was 120 million. I then began to meditate on this number and the Spirit began to move upon me. He brought me to the book of Jonah, chapter 4:11. "And should I not pity Nineveh, that great city, in which are more than one hundred twenty thousand persons..." He then took me to verse 1:17, in which it is recorded that Jonah was three days and three nights in the belly of the fish. This scripture revealed the number 3 twice (33). I correlated this number 33 with those Ninevites who were asleep at the time of Jonah's visitation to Nineveh, whose words of repentance saved more than 120,000 of the living. This totaled 153,000 living and dead Ninevites who were spiritually saved.

Now when I was about to apply this number to the rapture, the Spirit took me to Isaiah 60:22. "A little one shall become a thousand, and a small one a strong nation, I, the Lord, will hasten it in its time." I then took the number of those saved in Nineveh (153,000) and multiplied it by 1000, totaling 153,000,000. When the calculations were complete, the result was that more than 120,000,000, of the living will be taken up into the clouds at the time of the Rapture. Those who will remain asleep in Christ Jesus at the time of the rapture number more than 33,000,000. The Spirit then revealed to me that the 153,000,000 living and dead are the catch of the Apostles.

This number of 153 is recorded in John 21:11, when Jesus revealed Himself to His disciples at the Sea of Tiberius as they fished. As Jesus stood on the shore of the sea, he called to His disciples and said. "'Bring some of the fish which you have just caught.' Simon Peter went up and dragged the net to land, full of large fish, one hundred and fifty-three; and although there were so many, the net was not broken."

On that day of the Rapture, depending on the earth's population at that time, more than 120 million saints will be seen carried up into the clouds to meet Christ in the air. Those of the remaining six churches will walk through the remaining three years, three months, and three days until the time of the last trumpet blast, when the earth will be reaped.

The 144,000 Sealed:

Following the Rapture of the church, it is recorded in chapter 7:1 – 8, that one hundred forty-four thousand men of the twelve tribes of Israel will receive a mark on their foreheads. They will be sent out into the world as a testimony to Christ Jesus spreading the word of redemption to the remaining population of the earth. John goes on in verses 9 -17 about an innumerable amount of people from all nations, tribes, and tongues who are standing before the throne and before the Lamb. They were all clothed in white robes and held palm branches in their hands. "Then one of the elders answered, saying to me, 'Who are these arrayed in white robes, and where did they come from?' And I said to him, 'Sir you know'. So he said to me, 'These are the ones who come out of the great tribulation, and washed their robes and made them white in the blood of the Lamb'" (vv. 13 – 14).

These more than 120 million people, gathered from every nation of the world, will remain in the presence of the Lord until all the remaining plagues and prophecies are fulfilled upon the earth. Those of the remaining six churches will be tested by the trials and tribulations they must face and endure for the "name sake" of Christ Jesus. All who persevere through these times will be taken up into the clouds, on the arms of angels, to join those who were taken at the time of the Rapture.

One more seal must be broken before the seven trumpet blasts and the seven bowl judgments are sent and released upon the people of the earth. Woe to those who will be slain and killed by these plagues that are about to come upon the earth, who have not repented, and who are not raised at the blasting of the seventh and final trumpet. I say to you that it would be better for you if you had never been born.

Chapter 20

The Seventh Trumpet Blast:

The breaking of the seventh and final seal of the scroll is the prelude to the next group of seven calamities to be released upon the earth. It is recorded in chapter 8:1 that when Jesus breaks the final seal, there will be silence in heaven for about a half hour and seven angels are given seven trumpets. "So the seven angels who had the seven trumpets prepared themselves to sound" (v. 6).

Each blast of a trumpet will bring a new calamity upon the earth, spanning a period of three years, three months, and three days, until the seventh and final trumpet blast that will usher in the first resurrection of the dead and the reaping of the angels. This time period will also usher in the time of the Beast and the false prophet. Out of this Beast will rise a "vile person" who will be full of sinister schemes. He will go out to make war against the saints of God and the Lamb. He will also exalt himself above the Most High. He, as Nero before him, will come out of the four noble horns that are recorded in Daniel 8:1 – 14, 23 – 26. This is the "Little Horn" (also known as the Beast), the son of perdition—the Anti-Christ. During his short time, these seven trumpets will bring their calamity upon his empire (the modern-day European Union).

This first trumpet blast (v. 7) will cause a third of the trees and all the green grass to be burnt up.

The second trumpet blast (v. 8) will cause a great meteor to strike the (Mediterranean) sea, killing one third of its sea like and its shipping fleets.

The third trumpet blasts (vv. 10 – 11) and an angel comes down from the heavens who is called Wormwood. This angel causes one third of the earth's fresh water to become bitter and undrinkable. The fourth trumpet (vv. 12 – 13) causes one third of the sun, the moon, and the stars of heaven to darken.

The fifth trumpet blast (9:1 – 12) releases the locusts from the bottomless pit. These locusts will plague men for five months. They will be given stingers as the scorpion and bring much torment to those who dwell on the earth. Many interpret this description given of these locusts as possible helicopters of war as they go screeching over the battlefield.

The sixth trumpet blast (vv. 13 – 21) releases four angels who are bound at the Euphrates River. They will cause one third of mankind to be killed in battle. As the waters of the Euphrates and Tigris rivers dry up, the armies of the east will begin to cross them to make war with the Beast. Verse 16 records the number of the great army from the east, numbering two hundred million. An army of this magnitude is not an impossibility for the oriental countries of Eastern Asia. They will march down and across Asia, killing millions as they go. Their death machine will consist of the tank, aircraft, and heavy artillery. The multitude of their armed infantry alone (two hundred million with only their rifles, bayonets, and sidearm) would have the capability to level any army who might try to oppose it.

"But the rest of mankind, who were not killed by these plagues, did not repent of the works of their hands, that they should not worship demons, and idols of gold, silver, brass, stone, and wood, which can neither see nor hear nor walk. And they did not repent of their murders or their sorceries or their sexual immorality or their thefts" (vv. 20 – 21).

Those who were not killed in battle, did not repent of their ways, and were not taken at the time of the Reaping of the angels would be killed by the remaining seven bowl plagues. Following the Reaping, those people will go on to suffer for a short time until the cleansing of the earth is completed.

The Little Book:

Recorded in chapter 10, we see a mighty angel (Jesus) coming down from Heaven clothed with a cloud and a rainbow on His head. In His hand He held a little book. This little book is taken out of the hand of the Angel by John. He is told to eat the book, which tastes like honey to his mouth and bitter to his stomach. I believe this little book held the mysteries of the first and second beasts of chapter 13, and the mystery of the great Babylon in chapters 17 – 19. I believe this little book held these mysteries in it, because the voice again told him, "You must prophesy again about many peoples, nations, and tongue, and kings."

In chapter 10:4, John explains that when he was about to write the things that he had heard and seen, a voice came out of Heaven, saying, "Seal up the things which the seven thunders uttered, and do not write them". What was uttered on that day may never be revealed to us in either revelation or our hearing. However, the entirety of the events that were seen by John, concerning the mighty Angel who had one foot in the waters and the other on dry land, was revealed again in a dream vision by the same student who had had the dream previously about the percentage of people taken in the rapture.

He saw a Lamb with three of its four legs standing in the water, with one perched on the dry land. What he saw to be dry land is actually made up of large boulders heaped up on top of one another. On top of these boulders were two thrones, although they were fragile in comparison to the great boulders they sat on. Each throne seemed to be made of sandstone, and they were placed back to back with one another, one facing the south and one facing the north. The throne facing the south was unoccupied; in the other sat a man wearing a crown of a serpent on his head. The armrest of his throne was draped in the skins of serpents. This man, he said, was fierce-looking.

This second dream vision can be related to the event in chapter 10, of John and the mighty Angel. My interpretation is that the Lamb that my student saw is indeed Christ Jesus. The waters that the Lamb was standing in are the people of the earth, and the boulders of the dry land are the nations who will be ruled by this vile man who sits on the throne facing the north. He is the little horn, the son of perdition, who will make war against the saints of God and His Lamb. His throne that is made of sandstone and fragile in appearance will crumble quickly, for he will only reign for a short time. At the end of forty-two months, his reign will end and he, with his armies and the false prophet, will be thrown into the lake of fire.

The Two Witnesses:

"'And I will give power to my two witnesses, and they will prophecy one hundred two thousand and sixty days...These have power to shut heaven, so that no rain falls in the days of their prophecy; and they have powers over waters to turn them to blood, and to strike the earth with all plagues, as often as they desire'" (11:3, 6).

These two witnesses to whom John is prophesying are Moses and Elijah. It was Moses who struck the waters of the Nile and turned them to blood, and it was Elijah who prayed and stopped the rain from falling in the land during the reign of Ahab and Jezebel. It is recorded in Malachi 4:5 that the Lord will send Elijah back to the time of the end. "Behold, I will send you Elijah the prophet before the coming of the great and dreadful day of the Lord." The Lord also sent Moses and Elijah to Jesus when He stood on the Mount of Transfiguration. This was witnessed by three apostles of

Jesus: Peter, John, and James. "And behold, two men talked with Him, who were Moses and Elijah, who appeared in glory and spoke of His decease which He was about to accomplish at Jerusalem" (Lk. 9:30 – 31).

These two prophets of old will be sent upon the holy lands with a heavy hand to bring redemption to Israel and those who remain in the world. It will be a time of great drought and famine in the land. They shall continue on for 42 months until their time is completed. Then they shall be killed and their bodies will be laid in the street for the entire world to see. After three and one half days, however, they shall be raised up. "Now after the three-and-a-half days the breath of life from God entered them, and they stood on their feet, and great fear fell upon those who saw them. And they heard a loud voice from heaven saying, 'Come up here'. And they ascended to heaven in a cloud, and their enemies saw them" (vv. 11 – 12).

It is recorded in verses 13 – 14 that in that very same hour that the two prophets were taken up into heaven, a great earthquake hit the city of Jerusalem and killed seven thousand people... Just imagine the consequences of the heavens being shut up for forty-two months and no rain falling upon the earth the entire time. Millions upon millions would die of thirst and starvation all over the globe. The entire planet will become as a burnt dustbowl littered with the bones of the disobedient and impious.

Chapter 21

The Dragon, the Beast, and the False Prophet:

The Dragon:

John records a vision in chapter 12 of a dragon (symbolic of Satan), a Child (who is Jesus), and a Woman (symbolic of Israel). In verse 1, John describes a woman clothed with the sun (symbolizing Jacob, the father of the Israeli people) with the moon under her feet (representing Rachel, the wife of Jacob. On her head is a garland with twelve stars (the 12 patriarchs of Israel). The woman is also pregnant and in labor.

Then John saw a fiery red dragon appear with seven heads and seven diadems (crowns) on its heads. He records that the tail of the dragon drew one third of the stars in heaven and threw them down to the earth. We know these stars to be the fallen angels. Then he records that the dragon stood in front of the woman looking to devour her newborn Child. The Child, however, was taken up into Heaven, to the throne of God. When the Child was taken up, the woman fled into the wilderness, where a place had been prepared for her. She would stay in this place for one thousand two hundred sixty days (vv. 1 – 6).

When the Child Jesus was taken up into Heaven, a war broke out between the archangel Michael and his angels who fought the dragon, Satan, and his angels. By the blood of the Lamb and the word of His testimony, Satan and his angels were cast down to earth. "So the great dragon was cast out, that serpent of old, called the Devil and Satan...Now when the dragon saw that he had been cast down to the earth, he persecuted the woman (Israel) who gave birth to the Child" (v. 13).

However, the woman is given two wings of an eagle to fly into the wilderness (taken into the clouds), where she will be nourished for a time and times and half a time (42 months). "And the dragon was enraged with the woman, and he went to make war with the rest of her offspring [the tribulation period], who keep the commandments of God and have the testimony of Jesus Christ" (v. 17).

"Woe to the inhabitants of the earth and sea! For the devil has come down to you, having great wrath, because he knows that he has a short time."

The Seven-Headed Dragon:

The seven horns that wear the seven crowns are the seven rulers who persecuted both the woman and her offspring until the time the horn representing Hitler is cut off. The seven-headed dragon is depicted below, with horns representing: Augustus Caesar, Tiberius, Caligula, Claudius, Nero, Vespasian, and Adolf Hitler.

The Beast of Tribulation:

"Then I stood on the sand of the sea. And I saw a beast rising up out of the sea, having seven heads and ten horns, and on his horns ten crowns, and on his head a blasphemous name. Now the beast which I saw was like a leopard, his feet were like the feet of a bear, and his mouth like the mouth of a lion. The dragon gave him power, his throne, and great authority. And I saw one of the heads as if it

190

had been mortally wounded, and his deadly wound was healed. And all the world marveled and followed the beast" (Rev. 13:1 – 4).

(Post 2021)

This beast recorded in chapter 13:1-4, will raise up out of the ashes of World War II. We have watched its progression from the time of the Caesars to Hitler and the Nazi party. Seven great empires have risen up in Europe over the last two millenniums who, by force, have brought or united most of Europe and other territories under their control. The first and greatest of these seven was the Roman Empire, followed by the Byzantine Empire, Frankish Empire,

Holy Roman Empire, Ottoman Empire, the First French Empire, and the seventh and most fierce—Nazi Germany.

Germany, the seventh head of the beast, led by the last dictator of Europe, Adolf Hitler, attacked Poland on September 1, 1939, beginning the Second World War. During the course of the war, Hitler and his Nazi Party exterminated over 11 million people. Besides the Gypsies, Polish, and Soviet Slavs, who were systematically put to death, Hitler and the Nazi Party exterminated over 6 million Jews. The atrocities committed by Hitler and the Nazis during the course of World War II would come to fall heavily on the German people. By the final year of the war, the allied forces of the Soviet Union, the United States (who entered the war in 1941), Great Britain, and France had turned the war around and had Hitler and his Nazis on the run. On the date of April 30, 1945, with the Russians rapidly approaching his bunker in Berlin, Hitler, with his wife Eva Braun, committed suicide (Hitler by a pistol to his head and Eva by poison). On May 8, 1945, Germany surrendered and was divided into four military zones—The French in the southwest, the British in the northwest, United States in the south, and the Soviets in the east. This once-great empire and people were now being occupied by foreign forces and the German people's reunification had become a very unlikely possibility.

As illustrated above, upon the death of Hitler, the horn of the seventh and last head (Germany) was broken off. Between the years 1945 and 1990, the head was mortally wounded. On October 3, 1990, following the collapse of the Soviet Union and the toppling of the Berlin wall in November of 1989, Germany was now again a nation and a people.

Germany Unified:

The dragon in Revelation 12, was described by John as having the same seven heads and ten horns of the beast of tribulation described in chapter 13.Of the ten horns of the dragon, only seven wore the crowns of a king. The other three did not. The reason for the three bare horns is because their time has not yet come. To properly interpret this mystery, we must look back again at Daniel's prophecy of the Goat and the Ram in Daniel 8. The horn of the goat was broken off (the death of Alexander) and four noble horns came up in its place. This is the mystery of the seventh head of the beast (Germany). Upon the reunification of Germany, Helmet Kohl, the sitting chancellor of West Germany since 1982, became the first chancellor of the reunified Germany in the year 1990. He would be the first noble horn of the seventh head of the beast. He reigned from 1990 until 1998. The second noble horn to come up from the once wounded head was Gerhard Schoder. He reigned from 1998 to 2005. The third noble horn was, and still is to this day, Angel Merkel. If the fourth chancellor of the reunified Germany reigns a full eight-year term, the tenth horn of the beast of tribulation will not be completed until about the year 2021. This means two things. First, the Rapture will not take place until the ending reign of this fourth chancellor. Second, the dreaded Antichrist (the little horn), who is to come on the scene in the tribulation period, will not be revealed until the church is taken up into the clouds.

The Little Horn:

"So they worshipped the dragon who gave authority to the beast; and they worshipped the beast, saying, 'Who is like the beast? Who is able to make war with him?' And he was given a mouth speaking great things and blasphemes, and he was given authority to continue for forty-two months" (Rev. 13:4 – 5).

The prophecy of the little horn recorded in Daniel 8 is a dual prophecy. The first little horn, Nero, came forth from one of the four noble horns who came up before him, Augustus, his great uncle. The second little horn that is to come in the time of the end (the tribulation period) is going to come forth in the same manner—from the four noble horns that came up at the time of Germany's reunification. Like Nero's assault on the holy land and the Jewish people, this second little horn will come in this same spirit. He will seek to exalt himself above the Father of Lights and call himself God. He believes that whoever opposes him, such as the followers of God and His Lamb, will be persecuted unto death.

This final chancellor of Germany will exalt himself over the beast of the tribulation period, which we call the European Union, with his cunning and political influences.

History of the European Union (EU):

The European Union got its beginnings in the year 1951, under the Treaty of Paris, when Belgium, West Germany, Italy, Luxembourg, and the Netherlands became its first active members. By 1973, three more countries had joined: Denmark, the United Kingdom, and Ireland. Greece joined in 1981, and by 1993, this small confederation of countries became known as the European Union. Greece was followed by Spain and Portugal in 1996. The next three countries to join were Austria, Finland, and Sweden in 2001. The EU added ten more countries in 2004, bringing its number to twenty-five members. Its last enlargement was on January 1, 2007, bringing Romania and Bulgaria into the Union. The euro currency, introduced to the world market in 1999, has replaced the currency of most of the member countries. The European Central Bank was established on January 1, 2002.

Today, the European Union consists of 27 nations. By the time of the appearance of the second little horn, however, its numbers may be greater than our own.

The Beast from the Land:

"Then I saw another beast coming up out of the earth, and he had two horns like a lamb and spoke like the dragon" (13:11).

The Second Beast of the Tribulation Period

Who is this beast that exercises the authority of the first beast? It is the Vatican City in Rome. On February 11, 1929, a treaty was signed with Italy that made the Vatican City an independent state ruled under the supremacy of the Pope. This tiny sovereign state that only covers 109 acres sits over 1/6 of the entire world population. Over one billion people look to the Holy See (pope) for their spiritual guidance and salvation. The Pope, with his league of cardinals and archbishops, has both religious and political influence in just about every city, state, country, republic, and nation of our globe. It is my belief that when the church is raptured, those left behind will turn to the Holy See of their generation for answers and guidance through those uncertain and unpredictable times.

It is recorded in 13:12 – 18 that one of the two horns will rise up in this time and cause the world to follow the beast who had been mortally wounded and is now healed (the EU). This vile and deceptive person (the false prophet) will perform great and wondrous signs in the sight of the people. The scriptures reveal that he will even cause fire to come down from the sky. He will also give everyone who follows the first beast a mark on their right hand or on their forehead. "And that no one may buy or sell except one who has the mark or the name of the beast, or the number of his name" (v. 17).

All those who follow and worship the beast (European Union and the little horn) will be given a mark. Without a mark, whether it be on your right hand or your forehead, a chip inserted into your right hand, or some type of barcode to identify your citizenship or allegiance to the European Union, you will not be able to buy goods from the beast. However, in order to receive a mark, you will have had to worship his image and indulge in his immoralities.

"Then the beast was captured, and with him the false prophet who worked signs in his presence, by which he deceived those who received the mark of the beast and those who worshipped his image. These two were cast alive into the lake of fire burning with brimstone. And the rest were killed with the sword..." (Rev. 19:20 – 21).

To those who, in the tribulation period, take the mark of the beast and then look to repent and follow the true Lamb, Jesus says, "If your right eye causes you to sin, pluck it out and cast it from you...And if your right hand causes you to sin, cut it off and cast it from you; for it is more profitable for you that one of your members perish, than for your whole body to be cast into hell fire" (Mt. 5:29 – 30). I pray many turn from the beast in those final hours and do as Christ recommends. If it is by a retinal scan that you are identified as a member of the beast, pluck out your eye; if it is by a computer chip inserted into your right hand, cut off your hand. If it is by barcode on the hand or forearm that you are identified, remove it. To those who do defect from the beast in those final hours to join Christ in the air, I say this: your act of repentance will be as an act of treason to the beast, and you, with those who refused to take its mark, will be hunted down and persecuted even until death

666:

It is recorded in verse 17 that he who does not have the mark, name, or number of the beast cannot trade or buy from the beast. What is the meaning of his number? "Here is wisdom. Let him who has understanding calculate the number of the beast, for it is the number of a man; His number is 666" (v. 18).

For centuries, this number, 666, has been attributed to a vast amount of suspected Anti-Christ's, such as Nero and even a number of past popes. The latter were possibilities because of the words written on the pontifical crown: "Vicarius Filii Dei". This phrase is translated as "As the worshipful Son of God's Vicar and Caretaker, to whom the eternal divine will has given the highest rank of the holy church". I myself do not attribute this number to Nero or any past or future popes. The number 666 is actually the date and time of the Reaping of the angels. On the sixth day of the sixth month of the sixth year of the tribulation period, the final trumpet will blast, and those who sleep in Christ will be raised.

The number spoken of in Revelation 17 will be the individual's identification number, given to him at either the time of his birth or citizenship into the EU. This government number (i.e. our social security numbers) will be the tool with which the "image of the Beast" will also distinguish one European citizen from another. I believe that this identification number will not be 666, nor do I believe that this coming Anti-Christ can or will be identified by this or any other number.

Chapter 22

The Harvest is Ripe:

In the final hour before the reapers descend on the earth, Jesus will be seen on Mount Zion in the company of the one hundred forty-four thousand witnesses of the twelve tribes of Israel. These ones followed the Lamb through the tribulation period, having the mark of the name of God on their foreheads. They were sent out into the world ministering as witnesses of the Christ Jesus. They have now gathered on Mount Zion in anticipation of the reaping of the earth.

Preceding the reaping of the angels, John sees three angels fly in the sky. The first proclaims to every nation, tribe, tongue, and people of the earth in a loud voice, "Fear God and give glory to Him, for the hour of His judgment has come; and worship Him who made heaven and earth, the sea and the springs of water" (Rev. 14:7)

The second angel follows, saying, "Babylon [The Vatican City] is fallen, is fallen, that great city, because she has made all nations drink of the wine of her fornication" (v. 8).

The third and last angel then says in a loud voice, "'If anyone worships the beast and his image, and receives his mark on his forehead or hand, He himself shall also drink the wine of the wrath of God, which is poured out full strength into the cup of indignation. He shall be tormented with fire and brimstone in the presence of the holy angels and in the presence of the Lamb' Then I heard a voice from heaven saying to me, 'Write: Blessed are the dead who die in the Lord from now on.' 'Yes', says the Spirit, 'that they may rest from their labors, and their works follow them'" (vv. 9 – 10, 13).

In verse 13, the Spirit is speaking of those who defect from the beast and those who continue in Christ Jesus to the end. Many will be martyred in this time span of three years, three months, and three days until the earth is reaped. Both the dead and the living, who continue until the end, will be taken up into the clouds and will remain with the Lord in the air. They will be comforted until the final seven bowl judgments are cast down on the earth.

The Reaping of the Angels:

"Then the seventh angel sounded: And there were loud voices in heavens, saying, 'The kingdoms of this world have become the kingdoms of our Lord and His Christ, and He shall reign for ever and ever'" (Rev. 11:15).

In both 1 Corinthians 15:52 and 1 Thessalonians 4:16, when the seventh and final trumpet is sound, the dead, who sleep in Christ, will be raised with incorruptible bodies. We who are still alive, who keep the testimony of Christ, will be changed in a twinkling of an eye. Our old body of corruption will be changed to an incorruptible body and our mortality into immortality. We will be physically renewed to man's former state, as Adam and Eve in the Garden of Eden. Those who do not hold the testimony of Christ in their hearts will be kept in corruption. "...and the earth quaked, and the rocks were split, and the graves were opened; and many bodies of the saints who had fallen asleep were raised. And coming out of the graves after His resurrection, they went into the holy city and appeared to many" (Mt. 27:51 – 53).

This same event that happened in Jerusalem immediately following the resurrection of Jesus will happen in every city, town, and village, in every nation of the world. There will be earthquakes in every corner of the globe powerful enough to open the graves of the saints. Once the saints come out from their graves, they will walk among the living. Every eye will see the dead raised and will know that the end has come.

Jesus Coming on a Cloud:

"Thrust in Your sickle and reap, for the time has come for You to reap, for the harvest of the earth is ripe" (Rev. 14:15).

On this command of the angel, every eye, to the farthest corners of the earth, will see the Son of Man coming in the clouds of His glory with His angels. "Immediately after the tribulation of those days the sun will darken, and the moon will not give its light; and the stars will fall from heaven, and the powers of the heavens will be shaken...Then the sign of the Son of Man will appear in heaven, and then all the tribes of the earth will mourn, and they will see the Son of Man coming on the clouds heaven with power and great glory...And He will send His angels with a great sound of a trumpet, and they will gather together His elect from the four winds, from one end of heaven to the other" (Mt. 24:29 – 31).

Another dream vision was received by another student of mine regarding the reaping of the angles. He told me that when he received this dream he was in his early teens. This man told me that in the dream, he was in a city that looked like a war zone. Some of the buildings that had collapsed around him were reduced to nothing more than rubble. He could see people all around him looking up into the sky with their hands folded as if they were in prayer. Then he saw winged angels descending down from the clouds, two by two. Their faces were illuminated with the glory of God. They swooped down in pairs, one on the right side and the other on the left, and lifted the saints one by one into the clouds.

This is how both the living and those of the resurrection will be taken up into the air to be with the Lord. Those left on the earth will suffer, unto death, the last seven bowl judgments. These judgments will immediately fall upon the earth when the reaping of the angels is completed.

The Eight Percent:

At the time of the Rapture (the middle of the tribulation period), two percent of the living will be taken up into Heaven by whirlwinds. At the time of the reaping of the angels, an additional six percent of both the living and the resurrection will be taken up into the clouds to join that two percent. Therefore, eight percent of the world's population at the end of the tribulation period will be with the Lord in the air. This will be about four to five hundred million people, or one fourth of the Christian population of today. This correlates to the Parable of the Sower, recorded in Luke 8:4 – 8, 11 – 15. The Parable states that only one out of every four seeds that are sown in the hearts of men will fall on good ground and take root. In these end times, many will profess the name of Christ Jesus, but it is not what comes from your mouth that brings salvation but the true conviction of your heart. If your heart is truly receptive to the word of God, once the seed is sown, it will take root and lead you to salvation. However, if your heart is weighed down with the cares of the world with its pleasures and indulgences, the seed of the word of God will fall by the wayside and be gobbled up by the evil one. I say to those who walk through this time of the end to break up the fallow ground that is your heart and seek the Lord with perseverance and diligence. "But without faith it is impossible to please Him, for he who comes to God must believe that He is, and that He is a rewarder of those who diligently seek Him" (Heb. 11:6).

Chapter 23

The Seven Bowl Judgments:

"Then I saw another sign in heaven, great and marvelous: seven angels having the seven last plagues, for in them the wrath of God is completed. And I saw something like a sea of glass mingled with fire, and those who have victory over the beast, over his image over his mark and over the number of his name, standing on the sea of glass, having harps of God" (Rev. 15:1 – 3).

Those taken out of the tribulation period will celebrate their victory of the beast in the presence of God and His Lamb. They will also rejoice in knowing that the time of the beast is almost at its end and the earth will be soon purged of all unrighteousness.

The remaining time from when the earth is reaped until the last of the seven bowl judgments is poured out on the earth will be one year, one month, and one day. This remaining short period of time will complete the 84 months of the tribulation period. In this short period of time, the beast and the false prophet will be destroyed and cast into the lake of fire. Every man, woman, and child who had not been killed by the previous plagues and wars of the tribulation period will be killed by the remaining seven bowl judgments.

"Then I heard a loud voice from the temple saying to the angels, 'Go and pour out the bowls of the wrath of God on the earth'" (Rev. 16:1).

First Bowl:

When the angel pours out the first bowl upon the earth, loathsome sores will come upon all those who have the mark of the beast and on those who worship his image.

Second Bowl:

The second angel will turn the (Mediterranean) sea to blood (causing every sea creature to die) when he pours out his bowl upon the earth.

Third Bowl:

The third angel and his bowl will, in turn, cause the rivers and the springs of the earth to become like blood, causing men to thirst.

Fourth Bowl:

When the fourth angel pours out his bowl on the sun, the sun will begin to scorch the earth—every green plant and vegetation of the earth. Men will also suffer from its scorching heat.

Fifth Bowl:

The fifth angel will pour his bowl on the throne of the beast, and his kingdom will become full of darkness and men will blaspheme against the God of Heaven because of the pains, sores, and thirst. However, they will still not repent.

Sixth Bowl:

"Then the sixth angel poured out his bowl on the great river Euphrates, and its water was dried up, so that the way of the kings of the east [Orient] might be prepared. And I saw three unclean spirits like frogs coming out of the mouth of the dragon, out of the mouth of the beast, and out of the mouth of the false prophet. For they are spirits of demons, performing signs which go out to the kings of the earth and of the whole world, to gather them to the battle of that great day of God Almighty. And they gathered them together to a place called in Hebrew, Armageddon." (vv. 12 – 14, 16).

Armageddon:

Armageddon will be the final battle with the beast (the EU), his allies, and the opposing arms of the Orient. The name "Armageddon" is ancient Greek that is derived from the Hebrew *har meggido*, meaning Mountain of Megido. This future battlefield of the world armies is located approximately 25 miles west southwest of the bottom-most tip of the Sea of Galilee. Many battles have been fought on the plains of Megiddo tracing back as far as the 15th century BC.

At the time that the two-hundred-million-man army of the east is crossing over the dried up Euphrates River, the little horn will come up from the south to meet this massive army in the plains of Megiddo. This is what the prophet Daniel wrote of the Northern king's final battle and defeat: "But news from the east and the north shall trouble him; therefore he shall go out with great fury to destroy and annihilate. And he shall plant his tents of his palace between the seas [the Mediterranean and the Galilee: Megiddo and the glorious holy mountain [Zion]; yet he shall come to his end, and no one will help him" (Dan. 11:44 - 45).

It appears that when Daniel says, "no one will help him", he is referring to the fact that his allies will not come to his aide. Perhaps the sheer number and military might of the Eastern army is so overwhelming that they, his allies, might flee. It also could be that the alliances to be made by the beast will begin to wane as his conquests come to an end and his days become numbered. It shall not only be the beast and his armies who will fall on that great Day of the Lord; every army who comes to do battle at Armageddon will taste the wrath of the Lord. It is at this time that our Lord Christ Jesus appears on the scene, riding on a white horse, and on His head will be many crowns. With him will appear the armies of Heaven, clothed in fine white linen, riding on white horses. From His mouth will come a two-edged sword (the word of God) and with it He shall smite the nations. "And He has on His robe and on His thigh a name written:

King of Kings
and Lord of Lords"

(Rev. 19:16).

"And I saw the beast, the kings of the earth, and their armies, gathered together to make war against Him who sat on the horse and against His army" (v. 19).

Jesus smites those who come against Him in battle with the word of His mouth. The last plague that shall fall upon the beast and the armies of the earth is a nuclear blast. This plague is recorded in Zachariah 14:12 - 13:

"And this shall be the plague which the Lord will strike all the people who fought against Jerusalem:

"Their flesh shall dissolve

while they stand on their feet,

Their eyes shall dissolve in their sockets.

it shall come to pass in that day

that a great panic from the

Lord will be among them.

Everyone will seize the hand of

his neighbor,

And raise his hand against his

neighbor's hand."

It is recorded in Revelation 19:20 that following the nuclear strike, the beast and its army, the little horn (the Antichrist), and the false prophet will be cast into the lake of fire. This would mean that upon their physical deaths, their spirits will not descend into Hades but will be thrown right into hell's fire. "But I will show you whom you should fear: Fear Him who after He killed, has power to cast into hell; yes, I say to you, fear Him!" (Mt. 12:5).

With the armies of the earth destroyed at Armageddon, the seventh angel is ready to pour out the last and final plague on the remaining inhabitants of the earth. When the last bowl is poured into the air, a voice came out of Heaven, saying, "It is done!" "And there were noises and thunders and lightening's; and there was a great earthquake, such a mighty and great earthquake as had not occurred since men were on the earth. Now the great city was divided into three parts, and the cities of the nation's fell. And great Babylon [Vatican City] was remembered before God, to give her the cup of the wine of the fierceness of His wrath. Then every island fled away and the mountains were not found" (Rev. 16:17 - 20).

There are three major earthquakes mentioned in the scriptures that occur during the tribulation period. The first is recorded in Revelation 6:12, occurring at the time of the Rapture. The second is recorded in Matthew 27:51, occurring at the time of the Reaping of the angels. The third and most violent earthquake, recorded in 16:18, when the seventh and final bowl is poured on the earth. It will cause the mountains to collapse and crumble and the islands to sink back in the sea.

Why do such violent earthquakes occur in these final days of the tribulation period? I believe the reason for these great earthquakes is that the Lord God is beginning to break up the foundations of the deep, as He did at the time of the flood, which is recorded in Genesis 7:11. He began to break up the foundations of the earth at the time of the flood to begin the separation of Pangaea. It is my belief that He is breaking up the foundations again in the time of the end to now join the continents back together. This is not to suggest that Pangaea will be brought back to its original geographic location or its original form. However, I do believe that the seven continents will become one again. This will be explained in more detail in a follow chapter.

The scorching sun coupled with these great earthquakes and shifting earth, will bring uncontrollable fires upon all of the landmasses of earth. I had a conscious-vision of the earth in the time of the end, when it is burning with fire. I had closed my eyes one day for a nap, and as soon as I shut my eyes, a series of visions came to me. I looked and I saw the earth hanging in the heavens, as if I were standing on the moon. And I could see standing there a Man who had the appearance of a shepherd, holding a staff in His hand. Behind Him, on the top of the earth, I began to see what looked like trees rising up in a great abundance. Then the scene changed and I saw the top of the earth engulfed in flames, burning out of control. Immediately following that, I saw the earth again, but this time the Shepherd was standing on the earth with a great multitude of people behind Him.

I was unsure of the meaning of the vision when I first received it. I carried it around with me like a heavy weight until the scriptures were open to me. The apostle Peter also received a similar vision or revelation of the earth and its elements being purged by fire. "But the day of the Lord will come as a thief in the night, in which the heavens will pass away with a great noise, and the elements will melt with fervent heat; both the earth and the works that are in it will be burned up" (2 Pet. 3:10).

The vision and its purpose were then made known to me: The Lord will first come and take both the living and the resurrected in Christ Jesus. Then the earth and all that is in it will be purged with a fire. Once the purging is complete, the earth will be restored, and our Lord Jesus and those taken in the tribulation period will come back and reign on the renewed earth for one thousand years in peace and prosperity. This is the reason that those taken in the tribulation period are brought up into the clouds of Heaven–the earth and all its elements must be wrought in the fires of the Lord's indignation.

"Nevertheless we, according to the promise, look for new heavens and a new earth in which righteousness dwells."

I, myself, had a vision of a violent earthquake hitting the east coast of the United States.

Dream vision:

On the morning of February 26, of the year 2000, I woke to a prepared breakfast of scrambled eggs and pancakes. I ate, and still being tired from a restless night's sleep, I laid my head back down on my pillow. Quickly falling back into a slumber, I found myself on a beach face to face with the Lord. He was clothed in a white robe, and over the robe, He was wearing a tan coat, similar to the coat of a construction worker. He had His hands in the front pockets of the coat as He began speaking to me, saying, "I am not going to build My church here," as He spoke He took His right hand out of the front pocket of His coat and pointed towards the ocean, and said, "There is going to be an earthquake here." Then He turned toward the beachfront and said, "It is happening now." As I turned to face the beachfront, I saw a shocking sight. Every hotel and apartment building along the beachfront, as far as my eyes could see, was being viciously shaken. Every building was breaking in half and crumbling to the ground right before my eyes.

When the shaking seized I began to see people emerging from the rumble of the collapsed buildings. Then I saw others with what seemed to be walkie-talkies in their hands, and they began putting green army fatigues jackets on, such as the National Guard would wear. People were running frantically along the beachfront trying to help the victims of the earthquake. When I turned my eyes back to the Lord, to ask Him the meaning of this vision, He was gone.

I quickly woke from the vision and began writing down everything that the Lord had spoken and also my interpretation of the dream vision:

I recognized the beachfront as soon as I turned toward it in the vision. I frequented the Miami, Ft. Lauderdale area of Florida for many years, and I have no doubt that the beach I was standing on belonged to one of those cities.

My interpretation of the vision is this: The earthquake is going to hit off the Florida coast and a tremendous aftershock is going to devastate the southern east coast of Florida, during the height of the tourist season. I received the vision in February, and both the Lord and I were wearing coats in the vision, indicating that the earthquake will occur in the winter months.

At the time I received this vision, I, along with my family, were planning to relocate to the Ft. Lauderdale area. Needless to say, we decided not move to Florida.

Chapter 24

Babylon and the Beast:

In Revelation 17, John records seeing a harlot arrayed in purple and scarlet, riding on a scarlet beast which has seven heads and ten horns. On her forehead a name was written:

"MYSTERY,
BABYLON THE GREAT
THE MOTEHR OF HARLOTS
AND OF THE ABOMINATIONS
OF THE EARTH" (v. 5).

She was intoxicated with the blood of the saints (Jews) and with the blood of the martyrs of Jesus.

The harlot is a symbol of the Vatican City (the Catholic Church) post-Rapture. Some try to interpret this harlot as being the Rome of John's day, because of Rome's persecution of both the Jews and the Christian alike. However, the beast described in verse 3, whom the woman is sitting upon, is not the scarlet beast of John's day. This is the mystery of both the beast of John's day and the beast of the tribulation period: "Here is the mind which has wisdom: The seven heads are seven mountains on which the woman sits...There are also seven kings. Five have fallen, one is, and the other has not yet come. And when he comes, he must continue a short time...The beast that was, and is not, is himself the eighth, and is of the seven, and is going to perdition" (vv. 9 - 10).

In the days of John the Revelator, the beast had only six heads. John writes that out of the seven heads come seven kings. Five have fallen and one is. The sixth king or emperor who ruled Rome at the time John was exiled to Patmos was Vespasian. The five who fell before him were Augustus,

213

Tiberius, Caligula, Claudius, and Nero. He wrote that the seventh had not yet come. This means that the beast of John's day was not yet completed. The seventh head of the beast did not come until the year 1933, when Adolf Hitler became chancellor of Germany.

The eighth and final king/ruler of the beast will come out from the seventh head, meaning that the little horn (that is to come at the time of the end) will indeed come out of the seventh and last head of the beast (Germany), as recorded in Daniel's prophecy of the Ram and the Goat. He, the little horn, will come out of the four noble horns that come up on the wounded (seventh) head of the beast (Dan. 8:8 - 9).

Each of the beast's ten horns which wear the ten crowns will be a ruler who will rise up in the time of the tribulation period and will be given authority by the little horn to rule as kings. The people that these horns represent will rule as kings over the territories of the new revised European Empire. They shall also come to their end with the little horn and the false prophet at the battle of Armageddon.

The harlot will fall by the hand of the beast before its defeat at Armageddon. This was proclaimed by the angel in Revelation 14:8, before the beast is destroyed at the great battle of Armageddon. "And another angel followed, saying, 'Babylon is fallen, is fallen, that great city, because she has made all nations drink wine of the wrath of her fornication'".

The post-Rapture Catholic Church will sit as a widow during the final forty-two months of the tribulation period, but she (the Catholic Church) will say in her heart, "'I sit as queen, and am no widow, and will see no sorrow'. Then her demise will be quick and great. It will come on her in one day...death and mourning and famine. And she will be utterly burned with fire, for strong is the Lord who judges her" (Rev. 18:8).

The Lord will cause the very beast that carries her on his back to turn on her and destroy her. It is recorded that all the nations of the world will mourn for her, saying, "Alas, alas, that great city, in which all who had ships on the sea became rich by her wealth! For in one hour she is made desolate" (v. 19).

I am not trying to bring judgment on the Church in Rome, the Vatican City, or the Papacy with my personal theological interpretations. I myself come from a very devout Roman Catholic family and am not passing judgment on the Church of the past or the pre-Rapture Catholic Church. It is recorded in 2 Thessalonians 2:1 - 12 that at the time of the end, when the son of perdition is revealed, the Father will send a strong delusion upon the people, that they should believe the lies of the Antichrist who is to come. "That they all may be condemned who did not believe the truth but had pleasure in unrighteousness" (v. 12).

The true Church of Christ will be taken at the time of the Rapture and the Reaping of the angels. Included in these multitudes will be many denominational Catholic believers, for at the time of the end, a voice will come out of Heaven, saying, "Come out of her, my people, least you share in her sins, and least you receive of her plagues" (Rev. 18:4). Salvation shall come to all who believe in and stay obedient to the word of God.

Chapter 25

Satan Bound:

Following the battle of Armageddon, an angel of God will bind Satan with a great chain and cast him into the bottomless pit. This is where Satan will remain until the thousand-year reign of Christ Jesus has ended. Neither Satan nor his demons will be allowed to influence or deceive the saints during the Lord's millennial reign. However, as recorded in Revelation 20:3, "after these things he must be released for a little while." Satan and his demons will be released from their prisons, where they had been for a thousand years, to bring a testing upon those who walked with Christ during the millennium.

The Millennial Reign:

When Satan and his minions have been bound and the fires of the earth extinguished, Jesus and his saints will descend to the earth on the clouds of Heaven. The Lord will touch down on the Mount of Olives in the same manner that he was taken, and He and his saints will enter the holy city of Jerusalem. There Jesus will set His throne and the thrones of the twenty-four elders. We must remember the promise Jesus made to His apostles before His crucifixion: "Assuredly I say to you, that in the regeneration, when the Son of Man sits on the throne of His glory, you who have followed Me will sit on twelve thrones, judging the twelve tribes of Israel" (Mt. 19:28).

Once the thrones are set up in the holy city, Jesus will begin to call upon His saints as recorded in Luke 19:11 - 19,

"The Parable of the Minus". This parable that Jesus spoke to His servants was about His own coming kingdom, His triumphant return to claim His kingdom, and the delegation of His authority upon His subjects. "Then came the first, saying, 'Master, your mina [word] has earned ten minas [souls].' And He said to him, 'Well done, good servant; because you were faithful in very little, have authority over ten cities.' And the second came, saying, 'Master, your mina has earned five minas.' Likewise, He said to him, 'You also be over five cities'" (vv. 16 - 19).

Not all the saints who will enter into the 1000-year reign with Jesus will become kings, rulers, and lords in the kingdom of God. Those whose servitude to Christ Jesus goes beyond question will receive the rewards of kings and priests at the time of the regeneration. Many will rule with Christ during His millennial reign. This is why the name "King of kings and Lord of lords" is written on His robe and His thigh.

He will grant lands and territories to all those who will serve Him in the time of the regeneration. From the kings to the husbandman. All will go out from the holy city to begin a life of simplicity and peace. Men, with their wives and children, will leave the city in large caravans, seeking a new beginning in far-off lands. It is recorded in Isaiah chapter 4 that in the time of the regeneration the Branch of the Lord shall be beautiful and glorious. "And in that day seven women shall take hold of one man, saying, 'We will eat our own food and wear our own apparel; only let us be called by your name, to take away our reproach'" (Isa. 4:1)

These caravans will also consist of livestock–oxen, cattle, sheep, ass, and camels. Both domesticated and wild beasts of the plain will be preserved in the clouds, as they were in the ark at the time of Noah's flood. These animals will be preserved for the same purpose they were in the days of the flood–to replenish the earth. God's blessing to Noah and his sons, "Be fruitful and multiply, and fill the earth" (Gen. 9:1) will again be applied here, to the regeneration.

Man is to also replenish the earth and multiply upon it. Many Bible scholars, theologians, and eschatologists believe that those raised in the first resurrection will receive a celestial body form, similar to the angels', and will be unable to reproduce offspring in the time of the regeneration. They derive their opinions from a scripture that is recorded in Matthew chapter 22. When the Sadducees (a religious sect of the Jews) pose a question to Jesus about marriage and the resurrection, Jesus answers them, saying, "For in the resurrection they neither marry nor are given in marriage, but are like the angels of God in heaven" (v. 30). To correctly apply this scripture to the resurrection, we must first ask the question of which resurrection Jesus is speaking. The Bible clearly states that there are two separate resurrections. The first is the resurrection of the saints of Christ. The second resurrection is of the Jews and all those who sleep in Hades, following the thousand-year reign of Christ Jesus. Jesus was clearly speaking here of the second resurrection. He was not addressing gentiles, but Jews and the fate of those Jews in the second resurrection. Therefore, those who are raised in the first resurrection and given a new fleshy body will be capable, in their flesh, to reproduce offspring. This is unlike those who are raised in spirit at the time of the second resurrection.

As both man and beast replenish the earth, I believe that the continents will join back together as one super-continent which will again be called Pangaea as it was before the flood of Noah, and man will spread to every corner of the globe.

It is recorded in Isaiah 11:6 - 9 that in the time of the regeneration there shall be perfect harmony upon every creature that dwells on the earth: "The wolf also shall dwell with the lamb, the leopard shall lie down with the young goat, the calf and the young lion and the fatling together; And a little child shall lead them. The cow and the bear shall graze; their young ones shall lie down together; and the lion shall eat straw like the ox. The nursing child shall play by the cobra's hole, and the weaned child shall put his hand in the viper's den. They shall not hurt nor destroy in all My holy mountain, for the earth shall be full of the knowledge of the Lord as the waters cover the sea".

The nursing child and the weaned child shall be in those days. As the creatures of the earth eat the straw of the fields and the fruits of the trees, we shall also eat with them. The incorruptible flesh that both the living and the resurrected put on at both the time of the Rapture and the Reaping of the angels shall be nourished by the Tree of Life. "In the middle of its [New Jerusalem's] street, and on either side of the river, was the tree of life, which bore twelve fruits, each tree yielding its fruit every month. The leaves of the tree were for the healing of the nations" (Rev. 22:2).

As we walk with Jesus through His millennial reign our flesh shall be incorruptible and clothed with immortality, just as our father Adam when he walked with God in the Garden. By the Tree of Life, our flesh shall be preserved through the coming thousand-year reign.

"Blessed and holy is he who has part in the first resurrection. Over such the second death has no power, but they shall be priest of God and of Christ, and shall reign with Him a thousand years" (Rev. 20:4 - 6).

Satan and His Minions Released:

"Now when the thousand years have expired, Satan will be released from his prison and will go out to deceive the nations which are in the four corners of the earth, Gog and Magog, to gather them together to battle, whose number is as the sand of the sea" (vv. 7 - 8).

The mystery of why Satan and his minions are released upon the saints is explained. For a thousand years, children (who have not been tested) will be born to the saints of the millennial reign. Adam, the first man of the flesh, was tested in the Garden with his wife. Both he and his wife fell to the temptations of the serpent and were ultimately cast from the

Garden. The whole of humanity, at one time or another, has been tested by Satan. Kings, rulers, lords, peasants, and even the elect of God have fallen to his deceptions and manipulations. Even our Lord, after fasting forty days and forty nights, went through trials in the wilderness at the hands of this villain. Jesus' victory over Satan both in the wilderness and at the cross at Calvary made the way for our redemption and salvation.

So, too, must the children of the millennial reign (who will not be born under the curse of iniquity and sin but with a pure heart and incorruptible flesh) shall be tested. If both men and angels were tested and fell, then also those of pure heart must face the same wiles of the evil one. Those who are victorious over the devil will spend eternity with the Father and His Son. Those who fall to the wiles of the evil one, however, will be cast into the lake of fire that has been prepared for Satan and his minions. "They went up on the breadth of the earth and surrounded the camp of the saints and the beloved city. And fire came down from God out of heaven and devoured them [those who rebelled]. The devil, who deceived them, was cast into the lake of fire and brimstone where the beast and the false prophet are. And they will be tormented day and night forever and ever" (vv. 9 - 10).

Satan is released upon the Father's return from His millennial rest (Sabbath Day). Once Satan is cast into the lake of fire, the Lord will begin to carry out His judgment on all those who sleep in the darkness of Hades. This is the second resurrection of the dead.

Judgment Day:

"Then I saw a great white throne and Him who sat on it, from whose face the earth and the heavens fled away. And there was found no place for them. And I saw the dead, small and great, standing before God, and the books were opened.

220

And another book was open, which is the Book of Life. And the dead were judged according to their works, by the things which were written in the books. The sea gave up the dead who were in it, Death and Hades delivered up the dead who were in them. And they were judged, each one according to his works. Then Death and Hades were cast into the lake of fire. This is the second death. And anyone not found written in the Book of Life was cast into the lake of fire" (Rev. 20:11 - 15).

This great Day of Judgment will occur on the eighth day of man, the fifteenth day of Creation. Both Jew and Gentile will stand before God and be judged. This was the covenant the Father made with Abraham concerning his descendants: "He who is eight days old among you shall be circumcised...in the flesh of your foreskin..." (Gen. 17:11 - 12). The Lord also said this concerning Abraham's descendants after bringing them out of the captivity of Egypt: "so I swore in My wrath, 'They shall not enter My rest'" (Ps. 95:11).

Those who have not received Jesus as their Savior and Redeemer will not enter into the seventh day rest (Sabbath) of the Lord, and will be raised on the eighth day, "some to everlasting life, some to shame and everlasting contempt" (Dan. 12:2). The Jewish people are of the eighth day covenant, symbolized by the circumcision of their flesh. They were born under this law, and on the eighth day will be judged under this same law. Every tribe, tongue, and nation from the beginning of time will be judged with them. Those who are given to reign with Christ on the seventh day are of the seventh day covenant, the circumcision of the heart. These people will not be judged on the eighth day, but, on that day, will sit on the right hand of Him who redeemed them.

The Lake of Fire:

A third dream vision regarding the lake of fire was received by the same student who had the dream vision of the Reaping of the Angels. When he received this dream he was barely a teenager. The dream came to him shortly after the death of his father and that the dream was very disturbing to him.

My student explained that in the dream he was in the company of an angel, who was standing at his right side. He could not actually see the angel but the light that shone forth from him. The angel then walked with him down a long black tunnel that was as black as a cave. He began to see a light at the end of the tunnel. When he reached the end of the tunnel, he came to a massive cave. The floor of the cave was a river of molten lava. The walls and large stalactites that hung from its ceiling were engulfed in flames. Then he saw what looked like a man in the midst of the river of lava. This man was waving his hands in the air and screaming as if he was in agonizing pain. The river carried the man out of sight.

The man he saw trying to escape the torturous heat of the lava river was his father who had passed away months before. This vision of the lake of fire, which I believe was shared with me for the edification of us all. The vision may or may not be a deterrent to those who seek evil, but to those who seek God.

Recorded in Luke 16:19 - 31 is a story that Jesus told about a beggar named Lazarus and a rich man. Upon their deaths, the rich man was taken to hell and the beggar was carried by the angels to Abraham's bosom. The rich man, looking up and seeing Lazarus in the bosom of Abraham, cried out and said, "Father Abraham, have mercy on me, and send Lazarus that he may dip the tip of his finger in water and cool my tongue; for I am tormented in this flame" (v. 24). Abraham refused the rich man's request and said, "And besides all this, between us and you there is a great gulf [chasm] fixed, so that those who want to pass from here to you cannot, nor can those from there pass to us" (v. 26). There will be no escape from the hell fires, where Jesus said there will be constant wailings and gnashing of teeth and where their thirst will never be quenched and the flames will never cease to burn.

Eternity:

Following the great white throne judgment, the New Jerusalem will come down from Heaven arrayed in precious stones. On its foundations shall be written the name of the twelve apostles and on her gates the names of the twelve patriarchs of Israel. "The city had no need of the sun or of the moon to shine in it, for the glory of God illuminated it. The Lamb is its light...And the nations of those who are saved shall walk in its light, and the kings of the earth bring their glory and honor into it" (Rev. 21:23 - 24).

"Behold, I am coming quickly! Blessed is he who keeps the words of the prophecy of this book."

"I, Jesus, have sent My angel to testify to you these things in the churches. I am the Root of the Offspring of David, the Bright and Morning Star."

Revelation 22:7, 16

Epilogue

"Now learn this parable from the fig tree: When its branch has already become tender and put forth leaves, you know that summer is near...So you also, when you see all these things, you know that it is near–at the doors!...Assuredly, I say to you, this generation will by no means pass away till all these things take place" (Mt. 24:32 - 34).

Jesus spoke this parable to those of the first generation of the new millennium, about the year 32 AD. In the year 70 AD, the Romans besieged the city of Jerusalem and destroyed the temple, dispersing the Jews of the first and second generation (of the new millennium) throughout the empire. I believe this same parable can be applied to the first and second generation of this new millennium. Of course, no one knows the day or hour of His coming, but here Jesus assures us that we will know the season. Will it be the geo-political climate of our generation or the next that will reveal this coming calamity that is about to occur on earth? Or will it be the actual global climate, with its ever-intensifying earthquakes, tsunamis, hurricanes, and tornadoes? Perhaps the key to the mystery lies right in the most obvious place–the progression of the European Union.

The first prophesied little horn, Nero, came out of one of the four noble horns that came up on the head of the goat (Dan. 8:8 - 9). The second little horn of this dual-prophecy is to come out of one of the four noble horns (the four chancellors of the reunified Germany) of the seventh head of the beast. Nero came into power in the year 54 AD, forty years after the death of his great-uncle Augustus. Nero was also the fifth Emperor of Rome, who followed the death of the fourth noble horn of the goat, Claudius, his stepfather.

This second little horn (the Antichrist) may also become the fifth chancellor of the reunified Germany. He may begin his reign about the year 2021, at the ending rule of the fourth chancellor (who is yet to come). However, this Antichrist may also come on the political scene some forty years after the ending reign of one of the first four chancellors of Germany.

Perhaps Christ's second coming has no direct connections to either of these above scenarios. Or perhaps He will come back on the eve of the two thousandth anniversary of His crucifixion (which would be the year 2032). Another possible scenario is that He will come back on the two thousandth anniversary of the destruction of the temple of Jerusalem. There may be a dozen other possible predictions of the second coming of Christ Jesus. One thing we know for sure is that the day and hour of the Rapture of the church will come upon us unexpectedly, as Jesus prophesied during His Olivet discourse:

"Watch therefore, for you do not know when the master of the house is coming–in the evening, at midnight, at the crowing of the rooster, or in the morning...lest, coming suddenly, he find you sleeping. And what I say to you, I say to all: Watch!" (Mk. 13:35 - 37).

Made in the USA
Las Vegas, NV
16 May 2021